WRITERS SERIES

AFRICAN WRITERS SERIE[S]

Editorial Adviser · Chinua Achebe

74

EATING CHIEFS

EATING CHIEFS

Lwo Culture
from Lolwe to Malkal
selected, interpreted & transmuted
by Taban lo Liyong

HEINEMANN
LONDON NAIROBI IBADAN

Heinemann Educational Books Ltd
48 Charles Street, London WIX 8AH
PMB 5205 Ibadan · POB 25080 Nairobi
EDINBURGH   MELBOURNE   TORONTO
AUCKLAND   HONG KONG
SINGAPORE   NEW DELHI

ISBN 0 435 90074 9

PR
6062
I 97
E2

Set in Monotype Bembo
and printed in Great Britain by
Cox & Wyman Ltd, Fakenham, Norfolk

CONTENTS

Contents

ACKNOWLEDGEMENTS

To the Cultural Division of the Institute for Development Studies, University College, Nairobi, we owe this work. This was part of my research during my Tutorial Fellowship.

My gratitude goes to Professor Bethwell A. Ogot, the Director of the Cultural Division, Institute for Development Studies, for his invaluable encouragement, suggestions and for reading of these pieces in manuscript form.

To Dr Okot p'Bitek I also want to acknowledge my gratitude. It was in his home in Kisumu that the idea of writing this began. His books and suggestions helped greatly in the initial stages of the work.

And, of course, anybody doing research on the Lwo has to thank J. P. Crazzolara for his unorthodox, and yet detailed, research. Crazzolara is such a creative writer, readers acquainted with his work will not fail to see the extent of my indebtedness to him.

Finally, these pieces are common knowledge among Lwo and related people.

INTRODUCTION

'Lolwe' is the name the Southern Lwo gave to the greatest lake of Africa. This vast expanse of water had no end, it went *lolwe* – beyond the horizon.

'Malkal' is of course Malakal, the corruption of *Kal pa Mal* – the Palace of Mal – of the Northern Lwo in the Sudan.

Malakal is on the bank of the longest African river which the Lwo call Kir. This name we find in Jinja as Kira.

From Malakal in the north down the length of Kir to the bottom of Lolwe live a people. They call themselves Lwo. And they should be so known, rather than the 'dwellers on the bank of Kir'.

II

These are the Lwo sub-groups:

IN THE SUDAN Bor, Jo-Lwo, Thuri, Bwodho, Luo, Jur-Wir, Collo (Shilluk), Anywah, Pari.

IN UGANDA Acholi, Alur, Jo-Nam, Jo-Pawir (Jo-Palwo), Jo-p'-Adhola, Lango (culturally a mixed Karimojong-Lwo sub-group), Kumam (more Karimojong than Lwo, culturally), Jopawir in Southern Kaberamaido.

IN KENYA Luo.

IN TANZANIA A few souls on the south-eastern shore of Lolwe, the farthest Lwo migrants.

IN ETHIOPIA AND CONGO A few souls.

Obviously the culture of such a widely spread people is vast and varied. No comprehensive book could cover all of its aspects, let alone my forty-five bits and pieces.

What I have done is to select some representative works, pass them through my creative workshop, and present them in their transmuted form. I had an eye for those incidents which

lend themselves more easily to recreativity, through which
the soul of the Lwo can be explored.

I have been not so much interested in collecting traditions,
mythologies, or folktales. Anthropologists have done that. My
idea has been to create literary works from what
anthropologists collected and recorded. It is my aim to induce
creative writers to take off from where the anthropologists
have stopped. Greek dramatists based their plays on Greek
mythology.

Since I am dealing with folk literature, my only claim to
originality is in my creative efforts, my style, my vision, my
interpretations of the stories.

III

The history of a tribe is at the same time the history of the
other tribes with which such a tribe has had some dealings.
Hence the sharing of traditions and mythologies by the
Lwo with the other tribes in the Sudan, Ethiopia, Congo,
Uganda, Kenya, Tanzania (and possibly, Egypt).

Among the Lwo each sub-group has its own slant to the
same story. Some non-Lwo tribes tell the same event or
story, of course, with a bias.

The retelling of these past events is likely to touch on some
mini-nationalistic feelings. This is as it should be. After all,
Virgil did not agree with Homer's version of the Trojan War.
To live, our traditions have to be topical; to be topical they
must be used as part and parcel of our contemporary
contentions and controversies.

This book is merely an attempt to show what can be done.
If it inspires other artists or, better still, provokes them to
treat their tribal literature as raw material, or artistic forms for

containing their views on the past and the present, then our legacy from the past will have been accepted and our forefathers rewarded by multiplication of their efforts.

English Department   *Taban lo Liyong*
University College
Nairobi

SPEARS, BEADS, BEANS & OTHERS

The Spear, Bead and Bean Story

A man is not a man without his spear. With his spear he can
defend his own and win his wars and kill his game. In our
spear, our manhood resides. In our manhood, our spears are
found. A chief has his drums of rule. He must also have the
royal spear in which the collective might of his people resides.
If he loses this spear, the kingdom falls.

In the matter of Gipir[1] and Labongo,[2] we must remember
that both were princes. And according to custom, the most
capable prince is elected chief at the father's death. Some
people say Labongo and Gipir were twin brothers, but others
agree they were brothers. Whatever the case, Labongo had his
princely spear which Gipir in a hurry took to scare away a
bull elephant which was raiding his field. He speared the
elephant which ran off with the spear dangling from its side.
When he reported to Labongo the following morning,
Labongo demanded back his royal spear. Gipir argued
that his own field belongs to all. In driving away the
elephant he was ensuring plenty for all. Had the beast
been marauding Labongo's field, or any commoner's
he would have driven it away all the same. Labongo had no
ears for that. A royal spear lost is an omen for a kingdom
lost. Gipir begged to replace the spear. Labongo said his
magic resides in that particular spear: he is impotent without
it.

Gipir did not want to be responsible for robbing his
brother-contestant of a fair chance. Since he was still a man, he
could go and brave all dangers and, maybe, recover the spear.
His wives prepared for him some *peke*.[3] (He might have gone
with a follower or two.) After placing his case before the
spirits, he set out and was away a month or more on the trail
of the wounded elephant. Then he entered into a strange forest
and dark. To find that it hid the home of all the elephants.
There he found a woman as big as an elephant. In fact, one

could say she was *Min Lyec*.[4] She bade the stranger stop. He did. She asked him what he sought in her domain. Gipir said he had lost a spear brought hither on the back of a marauding elephant. The elephantine woman ruled: 'As the elephant has not yet died, and as you speared him while he was in the wrong, I shall give you back the spear. Otherwise, I would have had you killed.' Now that it was already evening, the elephants were assembling for sleep. She, also known as Nyambogo,[5] hid her guest in her hut.

The elephants arrived at this grandmother's house and said: 'We smell something. Men have arrived here today.' But they had no authority to question the Kind Mother. They went to their resting-place. At night when the elephants were sleeping, *Min Lyec* brought a bundle of spears. Gipir did not find the one that was his. Another bundle was brought and Gipir shook his head. The third proved the right one and Gipir smiled a little.

Nyambogo then urged Gipir to hurry out of the forest straightaway: if he slept in their domain they might kill him. But now that Gipir's *peke* was completely exhausted, Nyambogo gave him some *Ngor Lwo*,[6] into which, for some divinable reasons, she put a Chinese or a Japanese blue bead: *tiku Burjok*[7]: the hole or sore of God. In any case, the bead was oriental, therefore a gift of the magis.

[Royalty wears strange articles, especially Lwo royalties who have accumulated many strange subcultures in their wanderings. One of these royal regalia is a string of beads, blue beads. It strikes me as odd that a slit-eyed Chinese, labouring away under a stern mandarin, makes some blue beads for Chinese populace or peasants, and that these beads wend their way through all Asia, through north-east Africa, and finally this product becomes adopted by Lwo royalty for kings. (This *tiku Burjok* is also known as *Aba Mara*[8]: my father loves me.) Also that the blue bead should become a culture symbol, rivalling the spear – the spear, being itself an import, a foreign substance originating in far-away Merowe, or wherever it was, makes me say that when we speak of a 'pure' culture, we mean foreign amalgams nationalized.

[In any case, Gipir found himself favoured by the *Jok*-like[9] Mother Elephant: he was given the blue royal bead. If the spear symbolizes brute force such as was Achille's, the adoption of the far-travelled foreign blue bead, the beautifying article of culture-absorption, symbolizes the intellectual power for openness to the non-material, the progressive, and the new and foreign, among the Lwo.]

So Gipir walked home victorious: he had recovered his brother's manhood; he had been favoured with intellectual powers by the kindly elephant-child. He could now see himself resplendent in his goddess-given string of royal beads. He could also see his sons lording it over lands strange and peoples diverse. He would love to admire to be admired for the new acquisition which puts him a step ahead of his brethren: he'd enjoy to be the first Lwo to be so decorated, bodily, royally, and intellectually.

He returned Labongo's spear which Labongo stacked away more securely. The following morning he was sorting out his beads from beans. (There must also be beans for this mythically camouflaged story to attain full validity and dimensions.) That morning, one of his brother's wives came along with her daughter on her back to chat with her second husband: her brother-in-law. The child was naturally attracted by the beans which she started to eat. But the big blue bead attracted her more: more perhaps because of its enigma: that strange colour. Anyway, the little girl held the bead in her hand. Nay. She could not handle culture at a distance: she did the right thing: she swallowed it up. Thus was an intellectual

5

dimension added to Lwo life to rival the brute force of the spear, and maybe to transcend it.

Gipir of course demanded his objective co-relative. It was Labongo's turn to plead for a replacement: but the Magis visit us once only. Purgatives could only cleanse the eaten beans: the daughter vomited and had induced dysentery for three days and nights, and for three days and nights the bead did not come out. She almost passed her intestines out. On the fourth day, Labongo brought forth a knife and laid his daughter on a royal skin. He urged Gipir to dissect his daughter and recover his bead. Gipir refused, saying Labongo must do it, so that he would get the new blessing also. Labongo cut his daughter open: this famous daughter the mother of intellectual power among the Lwo, gave forth the new culture she had internalized for four days and nights. Everybody washed his hands in the blood and received the new baptism. Others walked the ground on which the rain water had washed this same blood. Everybody saw the recovered bead. (There is no tragedy here.)

And everybody dispersed to go and search his fortunes anywhere on the surface of the world. Some of them crossed the Nile on bridges of sudd, others might have done so in a historic period of drought when the Nile (or whatever the prototype river was[10]), was depth-bottom dry in places. Some of them went with their dogs and cows *tung piny* (southwards). And when they arrived there, from *yu malo* (up north) (up country) they fell like wonder, and were thought of only as a wonderful thing (*kintu*) who came from up."

The Lost Tribes

In the days of old, the clans of Panyiwer and Kalowang
Were the sole ministers of the customary rites of *Jwok*.[1]
They served their chiefs in that capacity.
To *Jwok* they performed the sacrifices.
The house of *Jwok* they always carried.
Jwok's very care and life they guarded.

Originally they were *jomiru kal*[2]
Whose functions embraced the clan
When it was yet big.

It is claimed the Panyiwer went with Gipir to return the
    spear;
It is claimed they preserved the spear after the brotherly quarrel;
It is claimed they also kept the knife with which the child of
    culture was cut away open, and when the oriental bead
    altered sense;
It is known that their number diminished;
It is recorded that the last Panyiwer has left the face of the earth;
It is believed they dried up due to the possession of those
    instruments so fatal:
As the Alur say: *tong ko pala odarogi!*[3]

But where the bead went nobody seems to know;
The *Ngor Lwo* still feeds out stomachs
Isn't the bead feeding our minds?

7

Nyilak, the Famous Girl of the Plains

When girls are beautiful they deserve to love:
When they are intelligent, they deserve to rule;
So thought *Rwot Lei*[1] over his only child, mind roving–Nyilak.
An order stern he meted out to her:
'To remain single you will ever be,
To mix with men, you will never do.
And when I die, to assume the throne.'
She promised she would follow:
(A mere act of mind without commerce with pathos),
A Lwo adage says: 'Girls slip away like fish.'
Shall we see an exception?

The girl of the plains Nyilak[2] became:
A herder of cows and sheep and goats, especially goats, she was;
Only the slaves herded with her.
Perhaps these thoughts were foreign to her;
Perhaps a slave could sate an urge;
Perhaps that would be too low a stoop ...
But every day the goats did it with distinction.

On a hot humid noonday, Nyilak resolved the dilemma:
A creature hairy[3] and strange emerged from the bush
His eyes were red and sweet, his odour was goat and hot.
Towards Nyilak this creature ambled forward: galvanizing all
    the air.
Nyilaak stood fixed; fixed down by that lustful stare.
(The beast moved forward and backward; Nyilak moved
    backward and forward.)
Then they rested; the creature went backwards; Nyilak went
    homewards
True to her promises she had never met a man.

They had not met once when they met many a time;
They had not met once when Nyilak's mind began to wonder:

8

Why should her chest heave so warmly?
And the cows and plains appear so full of beauty?
Her breasts were becoming fuller and her tummy roomy.
Was it the weather?
Old women shook their heads and said: 'Love is always the
    victor';
Old councillors dared not mutter as the bread at court was
    always sweeter.
Only the pied jester stuck to duty and said the chief had a
    grandson coming.

The great unknown decided it was time for revelation:
His real name he would conceal, but Ocak[4] was better;
As to *cako* indicates a beginning:
And an era vast and uncertain had its beginning right here in
    Nyilako.
But as he had not long to live and she would deliver just a pair
She had better collect his charred remains
And preserve them safe for power and Koth.[5]

'Who is her lover?' demanded her demented Rwot Lei.
And he waited long, too long for the answer.
And he had to search for that answer.
As Nyilak looked after her grazing cattle
The chief's men hid waiting ready for the kill.
When the strange-looking creature appeared Nyilak's desire
    soared;
Their minds said this is some *jwok*.
They dared not lift a spear.
But those who had fed much at court ensured their daily bread
And soon Ocak was dead.
– Dead to begin the biggest legend of Gipir and Labongo, his
    grandsons.

9

Gods Favour Those Born to be Kings

Lwo's son was Labongo
Labongo brought forth Kijok, Tereo, and Tika.
Rwot Labongo's end was drawing near
He wanted to be fair to his three children
The first child is just a child as much as the third or second:
They were all his intestines.
Since they were equally regal
He didn't care who took over after him.
But, since they were all able,
The election was to be done by chance and fate:
Whoever had the best luck or was most favoured by destiny
Would surely remain so favoured.

Three tests Labongo held in mind:
In the first he gave each son a cow
And asked each son to appeal to his cow
So that it brought forth a black bull-calf with a tail forked.
Tika prayed, Tereo appealed, Kijok entreated:
The calves came, Tereo's was brown, Kijok's was a female: only
      Tika's was fork-tailed, a bull, and black.
'Isn't this proof enough?' Labongo demanded.
Tika was quiet but his brothers were loath to submit.
Surely there were two more tests and two more chances.
This was just a battle: the major war was ahead.

For test two Labongo brought out a pot of beer
And gave each son a solid brass stick.
Each child was to suck the beer through his solid brass stick.
Kijok was first to try his luck:
He pulled and pulled, and thought there was a taste of beer.
He halted a while and found only bitter saliva of anxiety and
      rage.
He then pulled again but almost pulled his cheeks in.

– He gave it up in disgust.
Tereo tried his chance but realized he wasn't favoured.
When Tika sucked from his brass stick, that was another matter:
The solid brass stick hollowed itself of its own accord – or
    perhaps Tika's God did it for him –
Anyway, he drank beer all right.
The other brothers demurred and claimed Tika had hidden
    beer in his cheek before.

Olden Labongo was not in a hurry.
His third test would be the last:
Just as a baby boy is interned three days after birth
So a manly test has to be taken three times.
Two Madi spades he brought out:
Whoever strikes them against each other so that they stick
Would surely keep the people one.
Tereo the physically strong was sure of success,
So he grabbed the spades and struck them together:
Only a noise was heard.
Kijok, white with wrath, sought to confuse the election
And decided to strike the spades together,
Only to find he was further from luck.
Tika struck them together and made them unite.
'Separate them!' the enraged brothers demanded. And he
    did.
'Strike them again!' they again ordered. And he did.
He asked Tereo to separate them and Tereo walked away in
    disgust.
He asked Kijok to strike them together and they remained
    unattached,
Who threw them down and rushed away unbeating his father's
    declaration:
'*Tika aye laker-wu!* – Tika is your divinely chosen chief.'

11

Tereo went with his followers to Terego.
Kijok took his people to what is now Pajok.
Tika held fast and ruled his people of Patiko well.

There is an Old Kind Lady in Lwo Mythology

One sad morning an old kindly lady saw a young lady walking
by the river accompanied by her sorrow and tears.
She inquired of her what the matter was.
The sorrowful one related the following story:
  That she was a princess[1] who had a mysterious conception.
  That her father the king judged her children illegitimate:
  'My accursed twins[2] Opio and Odongo were given to privy
    commoners to suppress.'
  And that she was mourning their deaths and deciding to
    drown her sorrows.

  The kind old lady told her to dry her tears as she had some
wonders for her.
  They went into her hut and she rejoiced to see her own
babies growing up.[3]

[The children remained there but their mother came to nurse
them. After three years, the chief got wind of their inhuman
existence. He decided to co-exist with them seeing they had
refused to die. A sheep was killed as a sacrifice for their
reconciliation to human existence.]

  Odongo, born next, led his brother Opio in wisdom.
  One day, he moved to rule and pointed[4] his spear towards the
    chief.
  Then the chief died.
  Then Odongo[5] drummed his death and his ascension to the
    throne.

Ocudho of Kir

Cuai, Cuai[1] was our ancestor:
We are *Jo-wai*-Cuai,[2] we Anywah.
Kori, Kori-Nyairu was Cuai's famous child.

One day, boys or girls, went to fish.
Around a pool they sat catching fish with their hands.
A fish was caught by two children at the same time.
One said it was his and the other said he owned it:
A quarrel ensued, sides were taken and fishing was forgotten.

The River-man appeared: none other than Ocudho-Okiro:
He who lives with his wives in the river: hippos are his cows.
Ocudho sat on a log of wood in the river, watching them.
To save his ears from more shouts he had to intervene:
'The fish belongs to the child who held its head,' he declared
     and disappeared under water and the children went home.
The law-prone elders heard of this pronouncement and sought
     Ocudho for their judge.[3]
Next day a quarrel was re-enacted and Ocudho was caught
     passing Justice.

Cuai: Ocudho be with us! Ocudho *ling tik*.[4]
Cuai: Ocudho be my son! Ocudho *ling tik*.
Cuai: Ocudho own my land! Ocudho *ling tik*.
Cuai: Nyairu[5] take some food to Ocudho. Nyairu caught the
     path.
Cuai: Nyairu make Ocudho feel at home. Nyairu went and
     joked.

Cuai: Nyairu what is that? Nyairu saw her womb.
Cuai: Nyairu is Ocudho gone? Nyairu saw the river.

Cuai: Nyairu who is that? Nyairu: Just a son.
And that son was named Gilo:
It was he who started the Anywah royal dynasty.[6]

Rwot Lei

I like the way Jo-Okoro begin their genealogy:
They say their ancestors came from the north of the horizon.
And beyond that horizon, north of another horizon . . .
And they lose their north somewhere north there.

In that northern horizon there, they had a big chief called
    Rwot Lei.[1]
Rwot Lei was the son of Cua,
Cua was himself son of Acunga.
And Acunga was of course the son of –
– of nobody: no further ancestor is mentioned.
Arbitrariness rules the beginnings and the endings.

Acunga was born in a certain country full of animals.
In that country Mr Dog was the courtly messenger.
And the heir apparent, Prince Lion, was destined for the throne.
The extant chief was about to dissolve to earth
When he called Dog to transmit his breath to Lion.
Dog had grudges against the King-to-be.
So he sprinted to Acunga rather than his enemy-apparent.
The message brief and full
Urged Acunga to growl like Lion[2]
And report to the Chief that he had arrived
As he hid by the *kosika*.[3]

Acunga performed the play and usurped the crown.
He heard these dying pronouncements:
   'You shall succeed me.
   Look well after the country:
   Behold, I place everything into your hands.'
Then the chief died.
Acunga declared his ascension by beating the *Bul Ker*.[4]

Malkal, Kal pa Mal, Malakal

Mal[1] pricked his ears again.
'*Mal, e gu yen ne yoku?*'
Mal agreed he was looking after his cows.
(But the voice had come from inside a gourd, a metre wide, of
    Koth.)[2]
Mal ran home, all atremble. To his people he reported:
'*Te me gaya, te me rwac re ker:*
I am thoroughly upset, a man speaks from within the gourd
    there!'

Early next morning Mal rushed four oxen to the gourd.
Fifteen yards to go, the Gourd[3] commanded:
'Thou Mal, who cometh along, spear one ox where thou
    standeth!'
The ox was speared and it sought to die by the gourd with the
    belly towards it.
Ten steps to go another ox received the spear point:
It ran and fell belly-wise to the gourd.
Five steps and another ox exposed its belly,
Through these sacrificial deaths an omen was divined:
Koth had agreed to favour Mal.

Mal took his *Up-sent*[4] spear and cut the Gourd in two as
    instructed:
And Kany: *He that came forth*, got out of the gourd.
And Kany sat beside Mal alone.
Mal took the wonder child and brought him home.
The meat was left for the birds to eat and thank.

After Kany had grown a man
He decided to go south to *Nam*.[5]
But Mal and Kany exchanged some blood.[6]
For friendship beyond friendship:
Kany took Mal's daughter to wife.

Nyikango and Dak

Garo *wuad* Cang,[1] that is the son of Cang,
Was a rich man with many wives.
He decided to live in a country where Nyikango[2] and Dak[3]
    had to pass.
On one of his fingers he wore a silver ring which was visible
    from afar.
Seeing it, Dak was determined to bring it in his possession by
    all means.
The men of Garo lived along a river and by the side of a small
    lake.
Nyikango kept aloof:
Daak one day went towards Garo's country and came to a pool
    where he found some women bathing:
He wanted water, or so he pretended.
The ladies were annoyed at the stranger's intrusion and asked
    who this impertinent man was.
'I want water,' he said.
They told him they were of the people of Garo who would
    soon teach him a lesson.
Garo arrived. Fighting soon started.
Spears darted but missed. They came to blows.
In the end Dak threw Garo to the ground and cut off the
    finger with the bright ring.
Garo with his companions ran home to alarm the villagers:
While Dak with his followers drove the cattle of Garo.
Soon the men of Garo arrived.
Nyikango took an adze[4] and struck with it
Against the leg of Garo after some fighting.
The latter with his father Cang withdrew but drove their
    cattle before them.

[The *atego* (silver ring) remained in the possession of Dak and
reached Podhi Collo.[5] This famous ring, together with other

18

silver, was used to make a bracelet which is given to a Reth at his enthronement by the functioning members of the Nyikwom clan of Akurwa district: 'they are the seat of Nyikango – *ge ba kwom Nyikango*'. Only a *reth* may wear such a wristlet: a silver ring round the neck of a spear denotes the bearer to be the *reth* of the Collo.]

Nyikango and Dhimo

As they went fishing regularly in the pools along the Palugo
    river
They had to live on fish.
Dhimo one day bethought himself of playing a trick on
    Nyikango:
No reason is given for it.
He took a piece of *abobo* (ambatch wood)
And made it fish in size and looks.
He then placed it under water where he wished Nyikango to
    go and fish.
Nyikango arrived exactly there and speared it with an *abeth*
Or spike rejoicing in his good luck.
He felt greatly displeased at the sight of the *abobo* fish,
Evidently the *abobo* was prepared and laid on purpose.
Immediately Nyikango asked: 'Dhimo,
'Why do you play tricks on me?'
For fishing that day was at an end:
A hot argument arose and
    Nyikango's feelings were hurt.
He said Dhimo we are no longer of one kin;
Leave me alone and I shall leave you alone.
While they had in the past worked and lived together
Nyikango put an end to their relationship.[2]
The rainy season (*cwir*) did come
It brought plenty of rain for Dhimo
While it meant a complete drought for Nyikango.
'I am going to starve,' he complained
Suggesting that it was Dhimo who caused his drought.

Dak and Dhimo

Soon discord arose between Dak and Dhimo.
When everybody was asleep
Late one evening Dak rose from his bed and went to the
    water in order to fish.
Dak spent four nights at the river keeping under water.
Dhimo became alarmed at this disappearance of Dak and
    went in search.
'Anongo, where has Dak[1] gone?' Dhimo asked.
Anongo in all probability did not know.
Dhimo went then to Nyikango and said:
'Nyikango, Dak has disappeared.'
'I have nothing to do with him,' he answered.

Dak and Anongo soon came on the side of Nyikango.
They apparently went back by stealth.
Dhimo was furious about this double-dealing which amounted
    to treachery —
Possibly Dhimo had made important disclosures to Dak while
    he was on his side.
Hence his wrath now.
Dhimo the father-in-law decided to kill Dak secretly:
'Nyikango may live, but Dak must be speared —
Yi nak Dak!' But Dak was on his guard.
One night Dhimo's men followed Dak to his very village —
Ka ayode tok: but it was found that he was absent.
The pursuers, however, had been observed.
So Nyikango next day carved some *abobo*
To represent Dak in figure and size.[2]
At night it was placed in the courtyard, *dye kal*, where
Dak used to lie down.
Dhimo's men came after Dak and found him sleeping
Dye kal, and speared him.
Weeping started as 'Dak had been killed.'
Dak remained hidden in his hut:

Next day the lamentations of the people of Nyikango were
     to be heard.
In the morning Dak's *abobo* effigy was wrapped.
Cows according to the number of villages were held in
     readiness
And a big funeral ceremony took place.
Thuru, who had killed Dak came also.
Wasn't it his nephew's funeral?
The day of the funeral ceremony drew to a close:
Then Dak, unobtrusively left the hut:
Everybody was puzzled!
When Thuru observed him he ran away saying:
'What is the matter?
'Where does Dak come from?
'Has he not been killed and buried?'
Thuru saw that his secret was unmasked.
But he was utterly determined:
'Arms shall decide the issue.'

Early the next morning Dhimo was to come with his
     weapons.
Nyikango fled with Dak and their 'half-brother',
Gilo and with Dengdit.
They took to their canoes and made off
With them keeping always under water.
Thuru and his people pursued them
With their canoes, and were about to overtake them.
A slave then came before Nyikango and said:
'Spear me under water so that Thuru may go back.
'Otherwise he may kill you.'
The slave was pierced[3] and his corpse placed under water.
Its foul smell caused Thuru to break off pursuit.
He turned back. Thus Nyikango arrived in this country.

How Nyikango went to Heaven

Death-disappearance of Nyikango.
The popular conclusion of that story runs:
Nyikango, left alone with his Collo,
Became very tired of their unending feuds and disputes.
One such contender went one day and threw spear at
    Nyikango
Hitting him in the chest. 'Take me into a hut!'
He was taken into a hut, its roof opened by itself
And Nyikango went into the heights – into heaven,
In the shape of smoke – *keta mal a iro*.
The important chiefs were called
They entered the hut and did not see Nyikango
Because he had ascended into the sky as smoke
The members of Nyikango's family said to the chiefs:
'What are you looking for?
'Is he not up there moving towards the sky?'
Turning to the gazing people Nyikango said:
'My children why are you looking for me?'
Then he departed from them and went *mal* —
Into the heights.
He was never buried in the earth like ordinary people.
He sits by Jwok Atang[1]
Intent on furthering Collo interests, especially
With regard to rain. They very commonly pray
To Nyikango that he may do his best
To obtain from Jwok rain[2] and so on.
Jwok Atang himself is, of course,
Also approached directly and alone as the Almighty.
But the more commonly used praise is
'Jwok Atang *wuke Kwa* —
'Almighty God and our ancestor!'
Kwa is the ancestor: 'Nyikango.'

23

The Coming of Lomuku'dit

Who was king when they came?
Pintong the Great Rain Chief ruled us when they came.
Where did they come from, these beasts?
They came from nowhere, but arrived from the East.
What did they do to our villages, these hordes?
They burned them down, and robbed them hollow, these our
    destroyers.
And, to Liri the Hill, what did they do?
They burned it down with fire so that it threw no echoes.
And who were these, sackers of Bari villages?
They were the Lomuku'dit, our enemies – as many as grass.
What did Pintong do then, to save the land and his name?
He fetched Lokuryeji, the wonder-worker to drive away the
    locusts.
And what wonder did Lokuryeji do, to ward off this calamity?
He said: 'Chief, bring your magical sons Modi
  'Take one Modi to Pitya and let him go and thrust his
  'Iron Bar into the earth there;
  'Let the other Modi go to the West of the Nile with a man
    of the Minge clan and do likewise.'
Thus were these two men called Modi divided
And they broke off reeds from the swamps to use as spears.
The one dashed forward shaking his spear:
And the other did likewise.

What happened when mysterious Modi shook the spears that
    were reeds?
The forces of Lomuku'dit were completely broken,
Lomuku'dit disappeared to the west
And the land was saved.
Then all the villages which had scattered and hidden in the grass,
Assembled together again under the leadership of Pintong, our
    Great Rain King.

Part Two

EATING
CHIEFS

The First King in the World

If nature's call catches a hunter in the bush
And a *lacek*[1] comes running by
He is in luck as his spear or arrow
Will lay the proud animal low.

One day many brothers went a-hunting
The lame brother stirred a duiker when he squatted for health
The duiker ran for dear life as the brothers chased it for food
Till it saved itself by disappearing right in the kin of
     buffaloes . . .
These new meats were pounder than *lacek* and many in number
Inducing the brothers to forget their target.
'Let's catch these animals alive,' a voice shouted.
And everybody raced for a rounding
Till all beasts lost their freedom.
Then with joy in their hearts
And secured satisfaction, the brothers set out for home
All, all, with gladness.
Did I say 'all'? Pardon me, I am wrong.
One brother was lame, could not run, and owned not even a
     calf.
He had merely laid claim to the hill on which these animals
     were
And observed all that brawny scramble while his mind ran fast.
Now he ordered all the wealthy strong homegoers:
'Each one of you has made a catch;
But I have not a cow.
What I have caught, I have caught:
The land on which you tread;
The land on which your cattle move and graze.
As from now you will graze on my land
Whoever soils it with the blood of a cow
Must bring to me in sacrifice the entrails;

Henceforth, whoever spears a game or snares it in a net
Yields to me a back leg;
The man who kills in a hole, is quite a female and may eat all
    he catches.
During each harvest,
I demand a tribute of what my land yielded.
If you shed blood of a man on my land
You have to cleanse it with a bull;
Whoever kills an elephant,
    must bring me a tusk;
Whoever manages to kill a leopard,
    has to bring the royal skin to me;
After a waged war
I distribute all the spoils
Let there be no theft in my realm:
Or else the thief is fined a goat for a granary

To show your allegiance,
    and be permitted to graze and live on my land,
Straightaway now give me each a cow.'
The fast brothers unmaimed found their ruler there
Whom, being fast of mind, had circumscribed them all.
Instituting Kingship, ownership, and taxation.[2]

Apwoyo, Lagut, Ka Obi
The Hare, the Guy and the Ogre

One day Hare and Lagut went to hunt. At midday a heavy
storm broke out. Neither trees nor rocks could shelter the two
friends. Left and right they wheeled, up and down they ran, till
at last a ray of hope appeared in a thread of smoke. The
ten-eyed Obibi was busy in his smithy, manufacturing articles
of war with the help of his hungry-eyed sons. Lagut and
Apwoyo entered the mouth of the cave. Obibi and sons ogled
with appetites for lunch. Tiny Lagut and Apwoyo braced for
a war of wits.

In a voice roughened by the flesh and bones of men, the
father of destruction said: 'Ako! Ako! Strangers, you are
welcomed. Warm yourselves by my fire.' They sat by the fire.
He salivated. The guests were so plump and dainty. To sharpen
his appetite for the fresh supply of meat, Obibi pulled and
pushed harder at the leather bellows. Rhythmically, he sang in
a hoary voice about his luck that the smithy attracted food:

> 'Buk okelo yengo!¹
> Buk okelo yengo.
> Buk okelo yengo.
> My food has come.
> Moths come to burn.
> Own a forge and you feed to death.'

Lagut of the red breast begged their flesh-hungry host to let
them try their hands at the bellows, as this could warm them
up and boost high their spirits, now quite low. She began:

> 'Knock down the host
> Pin his neck down
> Pull the eyes out
> Eat the children first.'

Such an unlikely tune Obibi had never heard in all his gory
years. With eyes blazing in his head and temper at boiling

point, he snatched the bellows from the unknown guests: 'I
hate impertinent people. Sit mute by the fire and hear the song
my *nanga*[2] gives.' From above the firewood, and among
carcasses of men and beasts, Obibi extracted the *nanga* which he
strung loose and sang:

'My food came to my mouth
It found me seated on my haunches.
What luck I've got today!'

He sang for trials of nerves.

'Wonderful! Wonderful!' exclaimed the redoubtable Mr
Hare. 'Uncle, you play well and sing with elegance. But hand
over the avuncular harp and listen to a song of youth.' To a
high pitch the Hare's little fingers tuned the useful harp. A
highly-spirited tune he sang, giving the ogre the fright of his
life:

'Early in the morning yesterday
Didn't we have the catch of history?
Wasn't it big and bigger than this flea?
How easily shall we break these bones?
To skin that other lasted us half a day.
A weakling and a coward we have here.
Unless we eat this and double up his sons
Our lot will surely, surely be that of the hungry.'

And beneath his skin Obibi was a-tremble. 'Give back my
harp, you impertinent small thing, so that I may resume my
interrupted song.' The sinewy strings were unstrung. *'Bum!
Bum! Bum!'* Obibi strummed the floor of his den. The ten
eyes made the cave aglow, revealing to human eyes the empty
sockets of grannies whose eyes had vanished nourishing infants
of giants; and ears of elephants spread as the bedsteads. The
voice was now double-bass, and spit darted uncontrolled:

'I sat in my cave
And my food came to my mouth.
For years and generations, I have been ruler.
When all this talk is at an end, only teeth and claws will
    decide it.'

'If you are dependent on your wits you had better act fast,'
thought Apwoyo. He then said to Lagut: 'My cannibal friend
go and see where the rain is!'

The red-breasted Lagut returned to announce: 'The rain has
reached the forest in which we yesterday killed and ate the
fierce fighting lioness and all its cubs whose blood is still wet
on my chest.'

Then Obibi threw down the harp and tried to assemble his
scattered wits to find a way out. But soon Hare had tuned the
harp and Lagut pranced and danced gaily on tiptoes. With
wings outspread he swerved from corner to corner.

'How lucky some people can be in only two days to find
such a huge Obibi and all his fat sons at home. Surely Obibi
meat is always reputed the best meat. What a feast only two
friends are privileged to have? It's rather unfortunate that
Mrs Obibi is not present? Anyhow, when she returns, she will
be eaten for dessert.'

'Go! Go! Go! Go!' shouted trembling Obibi to his scared
young ones. 'Go and drive the birds away from the millet field.
But when you reach there, remember: Go and never return –
Lamanyi ki Ladwogi!'[3] The sons rushed out as if the den were on
fire. One child lost a tooth and another's upper eyes remained
on the cave wall.

In his composure, Hare asked: 'What was that you said just
now, Uncle?' And then the ogre swallowed fast and learnt
diplomacy and humility, saying that he had instructed his
sons to return quickly. Scarcely had a minute passed, while

31

Lagut and Hare danced for joy and Obibi trembled with fear, his eyes all a-droop and tail hanging low, before an excuse was made; the giant was afraid: 'I wonder what has delayed these silly sons of mine. I must just go and see.'

And only now did the door become too small. For the giant got the bruises and cuts only his victims had known; only now did he know stumps and thorns were powerful as he rushed insensibly through the fence and moat and the jeers of the birds.

Bilo Nyuka
Tasting Porridge

The Reli had no fire with them when they reached the Itula.
Reli sent his son to beg for fire:

'My son, get right every word of my mouth:
Go and observe the first words of the elders: the masters of
   the country.
If, says the headman: "How are you, my chief?"
Then you shall answer: "My slave, I am well."
Then add that I, his master, sent you for fire.'

Reli's son rehearsed this.

'On the other hand,' Reli said again
'Should he address you as "boy" or "slave"
You shall call him "chief".'

Reli's son, with a few comrades, then set out to look for fire.[1]
When the chief of Kagiri saw Reli's son and his retinue,
He was quite impressed, and met them with:

'Chief, how are you?
Where do you come from?
I am very pleased at your visit.
What can I do for you, my chief?'

'We are well as we hope you too are.
I come from the river side.
My father sent me to you, his slave.
He wants you to give him fire.'[2]

Chief Kagiri himself rushed to get him a chair.
His subjects offered fresh-caught fish to the son of their chief.
They also collected millet and beans, peanuts and dried meats

33

And carried all these to their new-found chief
With Chief Kagiri himself leading the way.
Thus Reli became the chief of Kagiri.
The Kagiri became the priests of court
And the pacifiers of land, sky, air and water.[3]

Kidnapped

Here we are, all Amwonyo and Avono: dying of hunger
And Baratogo cannot provide for us.
Here we are, all getting sick and old: signs of pain
And our chief cannot give us an ear.
Here we are, all commoners and children: together with wives
Not provided for by Baratogo the chief.
Here we are, all suffering of hunger: while Ter Agem
Food is enough and more.
Here we are, all bearing a thorny yoke: while Omyer's
    subjects
Live in heaven.
Here we are all envying others: while Omyer's sons
Lack people to rule.

Mustn't we a delegation send
To see how Omyer does the ruling?
To see if we can snatch a spark?

The scout went and ate with Omyer
Also.
The food that was left, went with the elders:
Also those at home must taste from the chief.
The guest from Amwonyo had his tummy full:
Gratitude swam within, and the head reasoned thus:
'Why are we drudging our lives over that shabbiness of a ruler
While here we have at hand a great *Rwot Madwong*?'
He asked for Omyer's son to escort him a while:
Magwar went with all respect
To play the host for good.

Behind the hill behind the home
Stalwarts five had Magwar up the air
Abduction had taken place:

(Payuda[1] was now at birth).
Omyer had lost a prince.
But to Amwonyo a chief was brought;
As Magwar was installed a ruler.[2]

The Path of Reason is a Twisted Thing

The path of reason is a twisted thing
So reason with moderation he who reasons.
At best fix a limit to your reasoning,
At least let arbitrariness rule your reason
Or else you will reason yourself out of yourself.

Omyer-dhyang-piny died when it was his time.
His throne he would have entrusted to Ndoro,
Who happened to have been his first son born.
But the majority of the people reasoned thus;
Motivated no doubt, by aesthetics:
'Won Angoro ecopo 'ngo ni camo ker'
'The hunchback cannot become a king.'
As if symmetry marked out kingship
And the hunchbacked is therefore bent double.
So frame-perfect Omyer was elected chief.
Spine-twisted Ndoro accepted the twist of fate
And, seeing disposition of his people, grumbled only in
        silence.

Now that the kingdom was lost, he sought for wealth
As a means of self-distinction and sorrow-extinction and/or
        drownage.
With cows he sought to excel, and would do it by crook and
        by hook.
The few cows he had, had their ears cut
And henceforth any cattle ear-cut belonged to Ndoro.
The common Lendu grazed their cattle in the common.
Ndoro's boys cut their ears and increased his stock.
Dry season came once, dry season came twice
Ndoro was the greatest cattle rancher alive.

Ndoro had a bull large and grave.

Although its back was straight, Ndoro's spirit was in it the
    more.
When he lowed, Ndoro sang his twisted heart out in praise.
When it delayed from kraal, Ndoro's nostrils refused to dilate.

Perfect Omyer also had a bull to signify his own qualities.
On a day intense with omens, the two brotherly bulls
    measured out their strengths.
They scorned the salt lick to straighten a hump or create one.
Omyer's bull was double bent double and died all at once.
Omyer felt his spine contorting, then stood up straight:
'Ndoro must replace my hero!' he declared,
'Even with his winning coward of a bull.'
Ndoro said no, at first because it conformed with tradition.
He said yes, after thought, he would supply a replacement.
Omyer's will was to prevail, so that very night
He supervised the robbery of Ndoro's bull plus other ear-cut
    bulls besides.
Ndoro's first wife was out with ache when the drama was
    played.
She neither raised an alarm nor reported to Ndoro straight.
'The cows had stirred for no special reason: perhaps it was the
    moon,' she replied with a twisted tongue.
Morning corrected the report and Ndoro cursed her once.
But she replied: 'Whoever reports a chief's misdemeanour?'
And Ndoro gulped for air.
'Besides, in the ensuing war my first son whose name I shouted
 . would surely die.'
Then Ndoro swooned away.

Robbed of might and wealth and respect
Ndoro removed his asymmetry to Got Jokia.
But he remembered his princely drum was still at Nebi.

To extricate this, he sent some people,
Only to find that the rock had decided with trees to embank it.
'Surely the very Gods have opposed its removal,' Won
    Angoro reasoned.

'Jwok ocere-re, wek edong gire'

'God detained it, let it remain there.'
And Ndoro's head sank into his spine.

Jo-Abira lived on grass:
Jo-Angal lived on beans;
Jo-Abira ate only wild fruits:
Jo-Angal cultivated corn;
Jo-Abira ate their foods raw:
Jo-Angal knew fire and cooked their foods.

Rwot Alal of Jo-Abira had lived for years and years in the
   peace and quiet of his ancestral domain:
Neither friends nor foes had paid them visits.
Rwot Ojangnga of Jo-Angal had roamed the lands and
   crossed the hills and rivers the way his Lwo ancestors did
   from time and place unknown.
Friends and foes he had met and dealt with them.
One morning Rwot Alal was alarmed by smoke drifting up.
The same morning Rwot Ojangnga wasn't alarmed when he
   saw messengers conducted towards his camp.
Rwot Alal wanted Rwot Ojangnga to report to him;
Rwot Ojangnga was not in a hurry and asked Rwot Alal
   to report instead.
(Napoleon dropped his glove:
Kutuzov picked it up for him!)
Rwot Alal's messengers carried messages:
Rwot Ojangnga's took *kwon*[1] as food as well.
Rwot Ojangnga's people did not accept the message.
Rwot Alal's wondered what to do with food.
Rwot Ojangnga's people hated the message.
Rwot Alal's tried food on dogs and hens.
Rwot Ojangnga's refused the message.
Rwot Alal's devoured the food.
Rwot Ojangnga ordered Rwot Alal to report to him,
Rwot Alal's people yearned for food.

Rwot Ojangnga asked Rwot Alal's messengers whom they
    would want for a chief.
Rwot Alal's messengers opted for food.
Rwot Ojangnga suggested they killed their chief first.
The messengers nodded and went away.

On the day of trial
Ojangnga told Alal to give up.
Alal said Ojangnga was impertinent
Alal's people shot first –
    right in the air.
And Ojangnga laughed.
Alal's one messenger shot again.
And Alal was dead.

Brightness is Itself a Curse

Among the *karani*[1] of the Chief of Padibe
There was one whose eyes were always red.
It was he who beat all his mates in smoking bhang
He smoked, and smoked, to get drunk – perhaps.
He smoked, and smoked, to learn forgetfulness – for sure.
But in the end the visions of curses ruined him.

Lokoya was this heir-to-have-been.
He could have died an infant if Mandala had not mercied him
That evening when Otto sat by the fireside
Carrying Lokoya on his back and singing out his life;
That evening when Otto's wives pranced by their husband.
That was the day Otto reviewed his bloody brave life
And Mandala almost shot him.

'Kaciba, my father, was a chief grand but not quite;
Jo-Agoro had raided us, and Lu-Atiak had raided us.
To wait for Jo-Ukaru to raid us now was beyond decree.
But we were weak and found no alliance near.
Words reached us that the Kutoria expected us;
And father sent Ladum Lawele to call for help.
They came and the Jo-Ukaru did not attack.
They did not remain alive, either.
Only then did we get respite.
Yet this was not for long.
One evening musket fire broke out and another power had
        arrived.
My father ran for life and hid in a granary.
Sir Samuel Baker pulled him out and drove Kutoria away.

'When my father was dead, it was natural I should ascend my
        throne,
Being favoured by the Arabs who called me Ibaraii;

And favoured by my father who called me Olorwo;
Also favoured by the Acholi who called me Otto.

'But my people ate their vomit and chose my nephew.
I would not have grudged Adot the throne but for my being
    made a living disgrace.
So I shot Adot and became a chief.
The Arabs caught me and I was taken prisoner in Ajulu: from
    throne to cell.
When I was moved to Padibe Rwot Ogwok would not see
    me rot
And forget there was a bond between us.
He pleaded my case and the Arabs asked for tusks.
My Oboo collected tusks, exhumed and green.
These went to Palodo and I was set free;
Favoured, moreover, with guns ten and Kutoria guards.
I had been stood on my head now twice: my people had
    shown the Arabs what to do.
What bond binds me further to friends and guests?
People complained I was cruel, but I was doing my work.
People complained I was unjust, but thieves must lose some
    limbs;
People complained I was unfair, but why must robbers and
    murderers be let live?

'One hot afternoon I wept to see a dance —
A dance I would not have seen if I had remained a slave:
I was slaved because my people by-passed me;
And I was a slave in the hands of these Arabs: represented by
    these ten slavers called my guards.
I ordered the Arabs be tied hands and feet
And ordered my slavers be thrown in the arena to dance a jig
    on their backs.

'. . . I wish I had killed them; I regretted doing things by half.
The slave dealers came and shot everybody on sight.
My subjects left me and also my freed guards.
My children died and away my wives went.
Even a Madi chief reproached me.
I embraced my fate and lived a commoner;
I sought to marry again and wooed two sister halves,
My father-in-law said no but more cows reversed the scale.
Lokoya, these are your mothers and always treat them well.
I understand there's a price on my head
But a chief can't be killed in vain.'

Just then Mandala fired a shot and Otto fell on the ground.
Lokoya dropped backwards, but to get up from the ground;
    unlike his sire.
Lokoya and his mothers mourned, but nobody else besides.

Mandala thought he was a hero, but not so the government
    which imprisoned him.
Mandala thought he was a hero, but nobody gave him refuge
    when he jumped the cell.
Mandala found he was an unhero as the blood of God's
    anointed drove him to death.

Types of Reasoning

'As I am chief, so I am chief and will so remain.
The people have chosen me one and lifted me above princes,
    and commoners are far below.
On this hill top the air is different and the view sublime.
My station gives me fresher and airier thoughts: only a fool
    would remain still common.
Now, the head of a cow might have been good meat for the
    people:
But they have the entrails and bones on which to glut:
The head will be burnt as incense to tickle my nose.
I have shoes, the land is mine, and where else can I walk?
I have shoes, the land is mine, what else can't I rule?
Sometimes flour is spread on my ground:
    I will walk on it to make my shoes white;
    to leave a kingly trail when I have gone;
Groundnuts spread on my land will change to music under my
    feet;
I am divine and man has no factor with me.
Any woman I meet will open her legs before me on her back
    when I feel the heat coming.
Any vultures that fly over my head will have a skull to peck;
    after all I have unruly subjects enough.
These weaklings now shall hunt by night and spend the day
    cooking and laughing for me.
Whilst a God has slaves, his wishes shall end fulfilled;'
    – So reasoned Awaza, King of Padere.

    – So reasoned the elders of Padere:
'Of long, a chief has to respect the women, the mothers of the land:
Of long, a chief has to respect the food, the gift of God;
Of long, a chief has to call for rain, the saliva for health;
Of long, a chief has to supply food and feast: part of what he
    owes to us.'

– So reasoned the elders of Padere:
'Most puissant chief Awaza of Padere
We kneel before you to beg for your shoes with iron and long
    hair:
The Panyonga who make them would like to fit you another
    pair.'

So reasoned the elders of Padere:
'Most respectful Keno, true prince of Padere:
We kneel before you to see if these shoes of iron and hair fit
    you well; . . .
Most fitted chief of Padere, we can see you are no longer
    young.
Most protected chief of Padere, we make and unmake in a day;[1]
Now Katulula beats on its own; it beats to mark an end.
That *kiling*[2] . . . *kiling* . . . *kiling* . . . *kiling ceng -du, kiling*
    ceng-du, jangiri okeng
Calls you to assume the throne
And reinstitute the reign of respect.'

The Birth of Kamalega

The baby had his fist clenched:
  He was born in Mukambo.
The baby had his fist clenched:
  His mother had come from Okoro.
The baby had his fist clenched:
  Kamarasi had sent her away.
The baby had his fist clenched:
  His mother was thought a slave.
The baby had his fist clenched:
  But Kamarasi had been with her.
The baby had his fist clenched:
  His mother was born an Alur.

The baby had his fist clenched:
  Only Mukamas-to-be are born thus:
The baby had his fist clenched:
  Please announce the news at court.
The baby had his fist clenched:
  Between him and the Mukama there was just a look.
The baby had his fist clenched:
  It was Kamalega who was born.

Obura the Just

A Lamogi girl was with child by an Agoro youth;
  Who was to pay the *luk*?[1]
The Lamogi parents should have taught their daughter;
  Who was to pay the *luk*?
The Agoro parents should have known better;
  Who was to pay the *luk*?
The girl's mother should have drilled her in chastity;
  But *luk* has still to be paid.
She should have known moonly abstention;
  What about the question of *luk*?
The boy's uncle should have married him a wife;
  But now who is to pay the *luk*?

Elders undecided. Chief Wira decided:
'*Jo-Lamogi ocul luk pay nyagi!*
Let Lamogi pay their daughter's *luk*.'
Elders undecided. Lamogi elders decided:
'The child will go to Agoro but we shall never pay the *luk*.'

The elders undecided, but listen to what a *Laloka*[2] had to say;
The elders undecided, but hear what the guest to Palaro had to
  say;
The elders undecided, but who is this unknown around?
The elders undecided, but why does he move from camp to
  camp?
The elders undecided, but what will our Obura say?
The chief misdecided, but in regal-source Bunyoro how is it
  decided?
The Lamogi half-decided, but let's hear the text from the
  Mukama's own son, Just Obura:
'The man pays the *luk*:
The child belongs to him.'

48

The elders decided: he who knows the laws must own the
     land;
The elders decided: he who rules with justice, owns our will.[3]
'Because of your intelligence, Obura, son of Mukama Olum
     Panya of Bunyoro, you become our chief right away.'

Dead Giraffe's Revenge

The giraffe: it is a tall animal.
The giraffe: its neck is tallest.
The giraffe: it is like a zebra.
The giraffe: its tail has black pearls.

The Lokoyo once wounded a giraffe
And it was Jo-Alero who brought it low.
The Alero claimed the right of kill:
The Koyo claimed its disability.
Rwot Obura said Lokoyo had a better claim:
They had brought down the giraffe.
To Jo-Alero he awarded the legs and the entrails:
The usual rewards for seconders and thirders.
The Alero took to arms when Lokoyo took the *wino rii*.[1]
The few unskilled Alero took to arms – and lost an age.
Onenge lost a son and cried to the lees.
Grief briefed him in the art and genius of retribution, so fierce.
He went to Panya Oluma of Loka Pawir:
(This very Panya had sought Obura's life
Omens and witchcrafts had divined Obura would be greater
    than him.)
Onenge, green with venom, sang the following tune in two
    tongues:

   '*Ayaa*[2]-Rwot, you sit here without a thought,
   Your son Obura plots day and night.
   Ayaa Rwot, your houses are so dishevelled,
   While Obura's houses are model.
   Maayaa Rwot, your doctors can't do a thing,
   Obura's surpass them by years and years.
   An do Rwot, your dress is *dogo*,[3]
   Obura is wrapped in furs;
   A million *oyo opilo*[4] compose his fur.

Wido Rwot, you are heavy with beads
Obura is adorned in tobacco seeds.
Eii Rwot you are so covered up
Obura's navel wears a ring . . .'

The sun reached up, the catalogue was still incomplete;
The sun went down and Olum adjourned the session.
Neither food nor water tasted he: the menu Onenge brought
     was full.
The song was too sweet and he doubted its veracity.
But the omens had favoured Obura, so he feared his insecurity.
Between belief and unbelief he had to flirt
And then at last digestion was complete
As he succumbed to flattery and what-will-people-say.
He made as if he was mad, jealousy swelled his neck.
Olum was white with rage.

Within a week mothers had donated all their sons;
Within a week the forces were filled by hundreds;
Within a week hundreds of miles were left behind.
Within a week Acaa was already laid low;
Within a week Jo-Paipeno were sealed in caves;
Within a week . . .

Obura dared not put out another force:
He was a man of sense.
The Palaro sought the summits:
Got Lute should give a refuge;
Got Lute would give the water.
But Got Lute had not the food
And Obura had changed the palace.
Beyond the Acaa he went with the guarders.
Under the mountain Oluma was breathing fire.

Up the mountain Palaro dropped some missiles.
Olum gaped in wonder, as the stones took his soldiers.
'Get some ladders,' Olum decided.
'With ladders you can scale this mountain.'
And his broken-winged ants built some ladders:
Lucifer's sons were posed for heaven.
With earnestness children thronged the ladders;
Battalion after battalion approached the summit.
And Olum belched and said: 'You shall see!' and rubbed his
        stomach in intellectual satisfaction.
And of course he saw:
The Palaro caught the top ends of the ladders
They heaved the ladders backwards
And all the soldiers perished
On their backs or broken-limbed.
Olum had lost the battle.
He turned his back to heaven
Tears distilled from his eyes
And he braced for attrition.

Soon enough food was finished,
And Palaro survived on water and anger.
Soon enough Obura heard the news,
And he decided to put an end to their suffering.
Soon enough Obura gave himself unconditionally,
And Panya became the victor.
Olum sat on a stool and Panya filled the other;
The dogs crouched around and the rock marked their places.
The Olum laid Obura royally to sleep:
A slave lay rock-above and the queen lay a-top o' him;
Obura lay on his queen with his eyes up in heaven;
Olum took the spike and thrust it down through them.

Bura Leb Bari

To the best of my knowledge
Bura[1] is a Bari word
Which has spread through the breadth and width
Of the lands of Lwo since encounter with Bari-speakers.

Jo-Padhola had a hero named Majanga
Whom Jwok Bura had had elected.

From the lowly position of milking Akore's avuncular cows
He won enough cows to get a wife.

He was a cowherd who was no mere cowherd:
Here was a cowmilker whom no angry cow wants to kick;
Majanga was a husband a little bit beside the herd:
Things were all straight in his home.

One day, Majanga went a hunting. Before they left the home he
    saw a colleague already writhing from python attack.
When he informed his friend, people said Majanga had lost his
    mind.
One day a girl was wailing to death six miles away from
    leopard attack.
People rushed there to see Majanga tell right again.
Rwot Akore had a big cow possessed of Jwok Bura:
Akore's rule lasted while he had that cow.
His rule ended when it went to Majanga.
People's respect moved to Majanga.[2]
Majanga's stocks increased as Akore's diminished more and
    more.
At long last Akore too was ruled by Majanga.
Possessed by Jwok Bura, he was feared and then blessed with
    obedience.
Through all these he wielded quite an army.

C

At a go he routed the Omoa who had fought them year after
    year.
He drove them all to Busoga.
Ensuring perpetual peace for all Jo-Padhola.

A Recent Occurrence

A British P.C.[1] influenced, no doubt, by Lord Lugard's
    'Indirect Rule' formula
Recently imagined the Kenya Luo should also have a king
So he set out to institute the idea of Rwotship among his
    people.
A working group set off for Uganda to witness the Baganda
    experiment in operation.
The group had some fun.
In the morning of the visit these Kenya Luo lined up among
    Baganda to see the Kabaka pass.
One Luo clerk who was not even a divisional chief
Was surprised to see people falling down on their knees.
'The Kabaka is coming!'
'The Kabaka is coming!'
He heard people say.
He looked up and saw no *Nyasaye*[2] coming!
'The Kabaka is coming!'
He checked the sky again and no *Polo*[3] was falling.
'Kneel down, the Kabaka is coming!'
He looked around and saw no frightening beast prowling.
'You enyagwangga,[4] *kneel down!'*
But it was useless now. The retinue passed alongside him and
    above the kneeling multitude.
The group's leader was a Lwo youth adorned in Arab
    costumes.

That day our clerk received from Bwana Pici quite an earful.
But inwardly, he could not see the awe or fright to make him
    bend on his knees before a human, a youth, at that.

However, things changed on the way home.
When they passed Busia our clerk had a Lwo dream.

When they reached Kisumu he urged the Luo to recognize
    him a king!
He sought to institute the proud dynasty of Owiny.
The dream of this Lwo who was not even a divisional chief!

Part Three

OK ICHIEM
GI WADWU

*Thou Shalt not Commune
with Thine Brethren*

Angulu

Angulu was the name.
The Lango went to war solely because of Angulu;
No part of Acholi escaped the invasion of Angulu;
To Alur Angulu went for war:
Angulu said Alur women bear twins:
'We shall have Alur mothers and Madi also.'
Angulu would not stay at home for a short while:
He must always be at war
He became fat by war
His life's business was war and the fame it brings;

And the praise of women it provokes
And the approbation of elders it awakens
And the aspiration of sons it inspires
And the tremble of foes it broadcasts
And the dread of Lango it brings
And the perpetuation of the name it preserves . . .

The Acholi said: 'He has a medicine against our spears.'
The Alur: 'This Umiru has a charm.'
The Madi: *'Lanyo 'di onzi; onzi; kanya kanya!*
These Lango are very bad.'
Beyond Madi he dared not go
As Iburu *a Lele* the strong rock of Kuku
Was a force beyond his reach.
But Angulu's name spread far and wide.
Angulu's spear struck here today
But tomorrow a mother far away is mourning another son
    dead . . .

Lango-Umiru became a tribe by Angulu;
Lango-Kide became allied in blood;
With such a horde Angulu roamed supreme

Thirsting for blood and fame.
When 'Umiru are coming!' is heard, mothers dress their sons
    in frocks:
Lamogi hide in caves.
Jonam truce with hippos . . .
But Patiko have nowhere to hide:
And that was their luck and Angulu's unluck!
It was a fateful night when Angulu and his band of braves
    camped in Patiko.
A cock crew, early, too early, at their back.
They moved thence, to find no village.
After a while a cock crew to the left
They hastened thence to strike the enemy dead.
A third cock crew and they thought they were now lucky.
The fourth cock was female and Angulu said: 'My luck has
    deserted me.'
Before they had hit a man, the Patiko *wuk wuk wuked*:
Patiko spears soon were finished.
Patiko women ran up the hill – like other women before
    them!
Angulu's insects combed house and granary for loot:
Cows and goats and sheep changed their owners.
Angulu breathed easy and looked for a fat ram to sacrifice.
When in a house he entered to get one
And held his knife to its neck
Then the Patiko royal spear descended
God-put and -propelled from Kibalo's hands,
And mighty Angulu was laid down low.

And, didn't the Langi give out such shrieks?
Didn't the Langi learn to mourn
When they saw Angulu was such an earth?
Wasn't it the bloody Langi who womanly cried:

Joni otuco nga ma?
Joni otuco Angulo ma!
Mai, Mai, Angulu otto oko ma![1]
Without a leader the horde was left.
Angulu was such a leader the Langi will he'd drained
To develop beside him and act as second in command was
      unheard of.
Angulu *Awimony Wontong*[2] gathered in his spear all the Lango
      manhood.
Panic-stricken, the Lango weaklings scattered like mad.
They ran for three days and for three days Patiko valiants
      stabbed
Only a handful reached home half-alive and women changed.
Peace returned to the lands and Lango remnants debated future
      revenge or none.

What form will the revenge take,
My muse please tell me that?
And where will it be done?
Will the chief
Through hatchet-prone intermediaries
Make bloody and hungry
Sections of the land?
Shall we have antiquated lawmakers
Breathing venom and fire in Parliament
Swearing revenge, as the Hansard didn't report?
Or will young stalwarts try their hands at penmanship
Or will would-be statesmen kindle fire by the great river
Though in our day of money and power
Bought advisers can prop up fools and idiots.
Or will young Achilles launch an Athenian attack
In a talk to young historians?
– This wrath of Achilles

Always begun because of a woman —
The spoils of war, grabbed by the best of fighters.

For, in every *atekere*[3] there are feuds. Little feuds.
Perhaps bigger feuds —
Since siblings fight to death
For the right of the breast.

There are more legacies our fathers left us
Than to harbour revenges for wars they fought or lost
About whose causes we do not know and shouldn't care.

It is meet and right
That each age should create its friends and enemies
Without the briefings of the old.
If we must perform a national surgery
Let's do it on a mourning day
And not originate a ground for revenge anew
By gloating and becoming fat
With the celebration of D-Day.

So long as politics lives
Exile and detention wait for everybody.
The Presidential lodges welcome and eject their guests.

If we must perform a surgery
Let it be done on a day of national mourning
And stop starting revenge anew.[4]

Kop Bino Ma Ikwiya
Fate Strikes without Warning

Slowly, the old man shifted from one side
His left leg rested on the mat;
His left elbow too was on the mat
But the palm supported his head.
The subdued night had a few thick clouds disturbing the stars.
The mysterious Got Kilak filled the distance.
The wind passed between the leaves of the trees without much
    of a stir.
His only son sat dutifully to listen to this too
Perhaps the last in the old series;
Cross-legged, the child sat, hands on the knees.

'All alone, your grandfather once went to war.
It was in the early morning when sleep is sweet
    and flesh would like to rest for good.
In the enemy camp the guards were snatching sleep.
With stealth he tipped on toes, four spears and a shield
    in his left,
Another spear on the alert he poised in his right.
To the enemy chief's camp he made his way.
To kill the chief was his intention.
To get a *nyi-moi*[1] was his commitment.
Five yards away he saw the chief.
He took correct aim for the kill.
And the spear –
The spear went astray: an ant had bitten his foot
And the spear killed the chief's aide.
And the ensuing stir killed his hope.
But another spear he darted and a man fell.
With his shield he dodged an enemy's missile,
A head fell foul of his *olayu*,[2]
As another enemy lost a life.

Through waking humanity he hacked his way:
Some woke up maimed, but others died in their innocence.
Blood and shrieks and cries marked his path.
The living enemies gathered in pursuit.
Your grandfather, the hero, ran for life.
He ran and passed the rivers five:
There were eight more to go but he was now tired.
Hunger and thirst made his plight hard.
Sooner than he expected, he was running in a dream:
His legs weighed tens and tons;
Breath refused to come
– And I am afraid he resigned himself to die.
He stopped, not because he wanted to.
A tree tall and straight stood by him.
To him he directed this plea:

"*Ayaa*,[3] you *beyo*,[4] you tree standing alone in the wilderness!
Have pity on another lonely creature.
My enemies are at my heels.
If indeed you are the tree my father planted
Help me, whom also that hand planted;
Bend down and whisk me up."

'Through his ears the *beyo* heard this appeal.
Suppley he lowered his pinnacle to reach his foot.
Your 'father sat on the only branch
And the *beyo* tree stood to attention.
The foes had ringed round the tree and now
With spears poised, sought the bush or grass
Under which they thought hid this lion.
But no secret hole hid your lion,
Nor was there a bush large enough to shelter.
Up the *beyo* tree their eyes climbed.

64

Dumb-struck, they stood, and decided to camp.
Hours passed and the sun decided to set
When "Wuk!! Wuk!!! Wuk!!!!",
Some enemies called in the distance, striking terror in the
    enemy.
"Wuk!! Wuk!!! Wuk!!!!" they called again.
From all around the cry for war came.
Nearer and nearer it approached the group encamped.
"Wuk!! Wuk!!! Wuk!!!! Wuk !!!!!" your father
    answered,
Giving the sign now well known at home.
"Wuk!! Wuk!!! Wuk!!!! Wuk!!!!! Come to my aid,
    Jo-Pacua[5]
Come and finish off these remnants.
Wuk!! Wuk!!! Wuk!!!! Wuk!!!!! Come in a hurry,
    blood-thirsty *Mony* Pacua."[5]
And wuk wuk wuk wuked the world.
The enemies below spread in disgust:
When killing is difficult it is better to keep alive.
They fled for dear life among the wuk wuk wuk
    approaching.

'After they were gone, the *beyo* tree lowered your
    grandfather down
And he took a branch to take with him,
And from the *okongo* bird who had cried the "Wuk!!
    Wuk!!!" he begged a feather.
Home he came and established the bond:
'This *beyo* and this *okongo* saved my life;
Henceforth no woman will make this a fuel.
Whoever cooks with *beyo* will never bear a child.
Let no boy kill the *okongo*,

Or else his mother goes blind."
My son,
Without your knowing this
You killed the *okongo* bird.'

The Ukebu, Iron, Meroe and Lwo

Among the Lwo everybody was a fighter, a hunter, a cattle
    keeper, a father, or a farmer:
Only the Ukebu knew the smithy.
They live among the Alur Mamalo[1] but speak their own
    language at home;
Their sole life was that of craftsmen by birth.
Every Lwo house had Ukebu earthenware or articles for the
    house or kitchen.
To forge all the hoes, arrows, knives, and spears was their
    monopolized field
As well as keeping it a secret from all others unknown.
Iron-work, they did and got paid for.
How the Ukebu learnt iron-work from far away Meroe, or
    whereever it was
Is still a puzzlement to social scientists.

The Birth of an Exodus

There are the Pojulu, and then there are those Zulu.
Are they related or not? That's a conjecture.

Julu and Reli were full brothers: that's for sure.
And each had an army of adherents: that cannot be denied.
They lived in a very hot country: that will become clear.
And had too much leisure: that was especially true of the men.
The land had little to give: so dissatisfaction, contentions
     abounded.
One cold morning the renowned blacksmith was busy
     hammering away at articles of war and peace and pride
When the public came, talked, and passed the day.
Other lesser artists were twisting ropes, making baskets, and
     other household goods.
Julu had his elders to the west and discoursed at length;
Reli remained with his in the east and talked and talked.
Meanwhile the sun moved.
Up and up it became, but hot and hotter too.
The Reli elders could not bear the barbs any more:
Only turtles die of bashfulness.
They begged the Julu to move a little and make some room.
Brothers begged brothers; brothers denied space to brothers.
'Why should we make room for people of our own age?
Let them stay where they are.'
'Never mind, let's endure it; the sun will not kill us.'
After noon, the sun moved west and the Julu were in for it.
The Reli rejoiced and the Julu gnashed.
The Julu sweated. They melted. They scowled.
Till they could not endure it any more.
'Please, brothers, move a little. We cannot bear the sun any
     more.'
There was smile and silence. Because they were fewer, they
     were content to smile in silence.

The Julu took their sticks and started prodding the Reli on
    their sides.
The Reli started shaking their fists at their assailants.
Noses were contorted left and right and poked right open.
As if that was not enough, the walking sticks struck bodies
    rather than the ground.
And these were soon exhausted, then wrestling became the trial:
And piti-piti-piti, piti-piti-piti feet stumped on the ground
    and men rolled other men on the dry ground.
The Reli had more foes to each of their men.
They tactically withdrew and hit with stones.
Soon, arrows replaced the stones and men fell with each arrow
    shot:
Sharp shooters now increased their stature.
All the Reeli were around, including women to collect the
    spears and arrows, and the children to learn for the future.
All the Julu were there to put an end to his junior's group.

After a while Reli moved for survival
Although it was in separation:

    'This kind of soil can be found elsewhere.
    Perhaps better land awaits the adventurer.
    We shall therefore leave you and go among strangers
    And struggle through life there.'

Excavation Sites

In Acholi there is a place and people called Lamogi;
They came from up north, from another group and place
    called Romogi:
It was from this self-same place that the Kenya Luo called
    Romogi came.

The Lamogi group came and settled under Got Kilak.
The area was not without people, though.
They found some aboriginals dwelling in the caves.
These, they called Jo–Boro.[1]

One day Lamogi had an *awak*[2] call and many peasants came to
    the communal dig.
They failed to eat all the sheep that were slaughtered,
Nor the *kwon*[3] that was provided; nor the many potted *kongo*.[4]
The work was also not complete when they retired home for
    the night and left their hoes by the field.

At night a scout from the cave-men came to reconnoitre and
    divine the day's noises.
His nostrils partook of the beer and he sipped a bowlful.
Mutton, cooked and salted, tasted so heavenly his captain
    despaired the gallant was dead.
And of course he was dead – with new experiences.
Curiosity filled up, he remembered duty.
The report was never fully given before the cave mouth was
    torn wide open.
Those cavers who met with *kwon* first, solidded their stomachs;
Those who took bones first, sniffed away in merriment Mount
    Olympus-like;
Those who grabbed flesh, had the best of food;
Others drank of the soup, and were filled with fat;

Some pushed their heads right into the beer and were drunk
    almost to death.

These godly feasts over, duty called.
Obviously savages and pygmies are all the same:
To them, the rule of fair exchange is the bond of faith:
If it is a pygmy who wrenched your plantain
You'll surely get a lump of meat instead.
After these cave-dwellers had had the food
They set to work, and cleared quite an acre,
After which they dragged drunks and drowns,
And repaired the mouth of cave.

The following morning struck the sons of man dumb.
'We can see for certain that the goblins still roam the earth!'
    they thought out aloud.
'But goblins may do the digging. Can they also eat some
    sheep and drink off beer?'
They deliberated long, had maxims many, and saged all the
    while.
The elders spoke quite a bit and the chief let the augurers talk.
The fruit of the day-long work was even this, that another dig
    be repeat;
And able-bodied men watch at night to catch the ghosts or foes
    if they failed to run or harm.

Human flesh fears pests, Lamogi watchers found this out.
The night advanced and the mosquitoes bled the veins of men.
Men who could brave the spears and arrows in the heat of the
    fray,
Men who fear not the smart of the canes or slaps of hands . . .
Men when they are enforced to quiet, become restless.

Men when they are entreated not to stir, find even their tranquil
    blood stirring, their soft skins pricking.
Now, when men have to be on guard for an enemy
And are not to show they are living
Better they were made Buddhists
Than bear such an ordeal.
No event took place whatsoever by midnight.
It was only towards three or four
That the earth shook to the onrush of the cavers.
Men observed their dress of wild leaves of banana *musa ensete*.
Men observed their eating as the decoy disappeared with such
    a speed.
And men observed all these sons, daughters, fathers, and
    mothers
Taking up hoes and deciding to be human.
And men could no longer stand the bites of the mosquitoes:
They took the cue from the beasts and rushed out to show
    some action.

The beasts fled to hell;
Human speed was not fast enough.
Only an elder with decades unknown had lost himself:
The others all went back to cave.

And man showed the prudence he had by sealing up the cave
In order to entomb the beasts for good, as if they had no sense
    at all.

Of course the cavers died – they died cursing.
And their ghosts committed revenge on Lamogi day in day out
To the extent that a while ago the Lamogi themselves
Had to open quickly the caves, led by the elder old

And run to beat the British who smoked them out or starved
    them[5]
Amidst the beasts they had killed.

My reader dear
If you do not fear ghosts
Go and make yourself a name
By excavating these grottoes
And finding out the civilizations
That are buried down underneath.[6]

Lacek Obalo Kaka

The *lacek*[1] is a beautiful animal but it also spoils *kaka*[2]
There was a man called Gicel who had sheep in plenty.
He had a brother who had no sheep at all.
Sometimes the Gods give problems to the poor.
Poor Atiko had his wife with womb.
And poor Atiko's wife brought forth twins.
And, as if this were not calamity enough, the twins were
      beasts, *nguu*.
Surely, Jok had made sure his powers were known.
Surely, these Jok twins had to be humanized.
And a sacrificial sheep was to be obtained.
Since tragedy had struck in stages two
And Atiko's Bari wife gave him twins and beasts,
He'd pacify the twinly stage that was known
And leave the beasts to prove themselves.

He'd have killed a sheep if he had one:
So he went to Gicel since he had none.
Gicel said: 'Your luck, dear brother, is your unluck:
The delicious white *ngwen*[3] have *okok*[4] for guards.'
Atiko cast around, and a brother came forward in the form of
      a friend from Ometta.

The unwanteds always excel and prosper.
And before a moon was up the *onyuu nguu*[5] had killed *anyiri*[6]
      for supper.
Atiko feasted and smacked lips for more.
Barely a six-month was gone when the brothers with claws
      felled a *lacek* down.
Atiko ate a week:
And a week Gicel waited in vain
For the brotherly *bat kaka*[7] which was surely his.
'Atiko, why did you eat the *lacek* alone?

Don't you know you have a brother?'
'I knew I had a brother,' Atiko replied,
'Till you refused to sacrifice me a sheep.
Then I knew brothers are born as well as made.'
Tongue-tied, Gicel moved away with his portion
And Atiko's sub-clan fed on meat and increased
Since most protein is in meat.
Atiko's sub-clan increased by tact, wisdom, and feeding,
Till it became Patiko.

[For the sake of laughter
Some people say that Atiko did not get a sheep at all.
He collected *lwaki lacene*[8] and sacrificed with them.
I don't believe it. But legally, since *lacene* have *moo*[9] just as
much as sheep, and since both are tasty – in fact the Lwo
royal clan in Buganda elevated *lacene* to the food of kings –
it is within reason, that *lacene* can be used in lieu of sheep!]

Jo[1]-Gem descended from Okulla, the son of Okwir, the son
    of Oraca, the son of Labongo.
Min[2]-Okulla bore him: *Won*[3]-Okulla is never mentioned.
Okulla left Laguti and went to Pajule to Rwot Gwara at
    Ngekidi.
Min-Okulla followed him later to go and stay with her sister
    or search for a male friend.
But she was already pregnant when she left for Pajule.
She had an affair with a subject of *Ladit*[4] Gwara at Ngekidi
    and she then miscarried.
No other child could she bear.
Okulla grew up and became the herdsman of Gwara.
One day Gwara called for Okulla but Okulla didn't hurry.
He called again and again, but Okulla made no response.
Messengers found him twisting a rope whose end he held fast
    with his toes.
Gwara was angry and remonstrated:
'*Unu ne itimo ki ngo ka?*
Itweyo kwede ki cuni?
Labong ata, dyangi mo pe ni!'

'What are you making a rope for?
Is it for tethering your penis?
Poor man, without a cow!'
Okulla was highly offended: he went and told his mother.
Min-Okulla told him that it was not her or his fault if
    he had no sister to earn him the necessary bride
    price.
Had it not been for that man of Gwara's group, she would
    have borne him a sister.
Moreover, he had a real home in Payira Te-Goma to which he
    could go if the abuses became too unbearable.
Okulla had his own ideas.

One day he was looking after all the goats and sheep of
    Ngekidi.
He moved off with all of them to Rwot Kijang *wot* Bito of
    Lokwor.
The Ngekidi people arrived in pursuit and asked for their *lim*[5]
    back.
Rwot Kijang gave the contestants a chance to state their cases.
Okulla's case was upheld by all the elders and chief.
The only things the Ngekidi got from Okulla were two goats
    for sacrifice to the *jok* of Ngekidi and a ram for the
    well-being of their children.
With his new-earned wealth
Okulla married Ajulu, *nya p*[6], Ogeny of the Lokwor tribal
    group
Then went home to Payira with his new young wife.
When he was about to step home with his wealth and wife
His mother rushed out and ordered him:
'Gem iyo wek kong gitum in!'
He halted outside the home and a propitiating sacrifice was
    made to the spirits.
Pien gugem iyo, likwayone gilwongogi ni Gem.
– Because they halted on the way home, his grandchildren are
    called Gem.[7]

Omera, Cip aye Otera Itim[1]

'Ah my brother, why do you treat me with such contempt?
You were born of my mother and father, so was I:
I was born first and should have owned this home
Alternating my name with father's in the tree.
Only that I have the *cip*[2] and you have the *com*;[3]
Why do you abuse my *tera*[4] as if *ter* have no use?
Wasn't I married because of my aprons?
Didn't I fetch cows because I am a woman?
Aren't you now married because of the dowry my apron
    earned?
Sure, a man can woo and win a girl;
Sure a man can dance and elope with a girl;
Sure the woman you bring home is called your wife: your
    property;
But why didn't you cut your *com* and take it for dowry?
Why did you urge me day and night to go and marry?
Who cried that he was growing old and a *labong*?[5]
I could not cook a meal, I could not greet a friend, I could not
    rest at night
But a hint was made about the debt I owed.
Now I went and got married and you are married too.
But rather than enjoy your wedding bed, you have changed
    the tune:
It is *ter* Abwoc[6] your tongue must abuse.
I will now go away where I shall be in peace.'

To you Crazzolara

Kec Nguu[1] drove the Patiko to Payira.

They were not refused, but allowed to stay.

After a while Rwot Loni reminded the Patiko that he wanted his customary tributes from his new subjects.

Okello-woro of Patiko said: 'How come? We have not joined Lu-Payira: we are just temporary residents while this famine lasts.'

Rwot Loni then said: 'All right, but whatever game your youth kills must be offered to me.'

Okello-woro retreated with his elders and said: 'I see clearly that we are being driven off or starved to death. Only our young men can hunt and kill the big game; our elders are too stiff-jointed to run after the big animals. My people, what shall we do?' From the advice given the following resolutions were made: 'As hunger still sways us, we have to submit – in a way. Whenever a young man kills a large animal like the elephant, giraffe, hippo, buffalo, rhino, lion, or leopard for which a *tyer*[2] is due the chief, the young man shall not blow his whistle to indicate that he has killed the beast: an elder or his elder brother shall, instead. But whenever a young man kills a rat, he shall whistle up to heaven.'

After six months Loni shook his head and could swallow only his saliva: 'Among us, the young men kill the animals, but it is your elders who kill the game.'

The Patiko elders chuckled: Rwot Loni had not understood their *Dum Patiko*[3] at all.

Kalabara's Damp Sore

On account, he said, of bad sore
Kalabara brought with himself a carefully bandaged leg.
The Rwot of Lamogi kept him a day but not one night;
His wives had more to do than provide water for a stranger's
    evil-smelling sore.
Chief Wira showed his heart by sending Kalabara to Chief
    Ojoko.
Ojoko showed his breeding by accepting the sored man.
His wives showed their upbringing by welcoming the care of
    the leg.

But what a sore was this?
It never smelled, though the bandage was damp:
Flies had no business flitting around it;
The owner never groaned even once;
He was never seen dressing it. Now, what was it?
He only squeezed the bandage once in a while and then water
    covered the ground beneath.
Having gauged the Rwot's heart equal to his wives',
Their actions matching their desires,
Kalabara one day paid like with like.
The leg he undressed and gave its contents to the chief:
The Rain-making power of Pabo.

The Division of Labour among the Pari

The Pari[1] are five to six feet tall
And of slight build as befits their mode of life.
They pay greater attention to the location of work for women
    than any other tribe I have met:
They give as reason that women are precious among them
As it would not be easy to find the number of females which
    would be required by such a population:
They are therefore doing their best to spare and preserve them.[2]

Man's share of work:
Men have to do the entire field work, that is:
Clearing the land selected for cultivation from grass or dura
    stacks from the previous crop;
Men prepare the field and dig holes with a sharpened pole into
    which women and children drop seeds;
Easy work, that, but it has to be done quickly and immediately
    after a good rain has conveniently soaked the ground;
Men have to do the important but patient work of weeding
    and harvesting;
Men have to provide the material for, and erect, the platforms
    in the fields from which the boys scare away the large
    swarms of birds which appear when the corn is about to
    ripen;
Men have to supply beams, poles, and stalks of all sizes required
    for hut building;
They have to cut and carry the grass for thatching the roof
Besides preparing the necessary quantity of ropes –
Long and tedious tasks.
The actual building of the hut is entirely man's work
As well as the cutting of stalks and posts for the courtyard
    fence
And putting it up and keeping it in good repair.

81

Woman's share of the work:
The women here are between five and six feet tall.
But they have more difficulty in getting into houses.
They can only prepare the threshing-floor in the field by
    beating and levelling it;
They can only thresh the corn, carry it home, and pour it into
    the granary;
They have to provide fire-wood and water for cooking and
    drinking.
When food is scarce they can only collect edible fruits like
    cwa, thou or *cum.*
Some roots such as *atwoli* are likewise dug for food.
It is women's work to beat flat and keep smooth the floor of
    the hut and courtyard:
Those are the only things the women of Pari must do.
Besides, nobody beats them.

Women love Jo-Pari.
I was told that there are at Lepul, that is the land of the
    Pari,
A good number of women captured during raids in different
    countries.
They could easily go back now if they wanted to.
But they have no idea of doing so.
No, no, siree:
Their condition among the Pari is better than in any other
    home.

Yom Cwiny Oneko[1] Latina

[The only thing to stop beer tasting like porridge is to put yeast
into it. This Latina discovered in her scientific mind after
observing the strength of taproots. In her classified way, she
added humidity to the millet grains and had them impregnated.
Within a day or two the grains burst open with life and the
potent roots shot downwards. Latina arrested the energy
wastage and had the sun fast blight the burst grains and roots.
She ground the intrapped energy and added it into the alcohol-
less beer. Then Latina hefted, rushed her new concoction with
pleasure to her chief.]

Cwa Mero was the chief when Latina died, poor Latina.
Kongo[2] had been made without *tobi*[3] till Latina came, poor Latina.
The new invention must be taken to the chief, so thought Latina.
Imbued with respect for her chief, and with beer on her head,
    she arrived at the palace a stranger, poor Latina.
The chief took one swig and said: 'Latina, give me more!'
    Loving Latina.
An *awal-pong*[4] he drank non-stop till down he fell dead, potent
Latina.
– Or so thought the people who beat her dead, dead Latina.

A chief cannot be killed for nought, they should know
Royalty can be entertained but only with the tried and proved,
    as is everywhere the norm:
Chiefs are not for experimentation, that's the rule.
Although they may experiment, that's their privilege from
    ages past.
They killed you for fear you'd killed their chief, poor Latina.
The chief later woke from his first drunkenness, cold Latina.
– And the remaining beer he drank in your memory, our
    bright proverbed Latina.[5]

Luwang Lwak

Among them there is a group called *luwang lwak*:[1]
These are they who guard the traditional good old customs
As well as the newly concocted institutions being pushed with
   vigour.
And they do it very effectively:
Any infringement that is reported is duly and unrelentlessly
   punished;

[Sometimes they search out for infringements by listening and
looking everywhere, taking photographs, and tape records,
bribing friends to get betrayers, torturing and blackmailing
others to extort information, opening people's hearts through
the use of beer, or making love to women to get soft
information.]

Say a woman is found misbehaved . . .
A delegation from *Longotyer*,[2] that is *luwang lwak*, will suddenly
   appear in her courtyard
And administer the deserved thrashing that she and her
   neighbours will not forget.
(Whether her guilty partner gets a similar equally deserved
   treatment was not mentioned to me,
However, it is possible for the partner to go scot-free if his
   eyes are big or his kraal full.)
Anything done against the decision or permission of the
   Longotyer is liable to thorough punishment,
As the *Longotyer* also punish for private grudges in the name
   of the *Lwak*.
It definitely acts as a deterrent to people.

I got the impression that this kind of institution may sometimes
   lead to acts of arrogance.
On frequent occasions when I was going along

84

I saw the *Longotyer* sitting together in a conspicuous place up
    the mountain slope.
At other times I identified one who was raggedly dressed
    drinking with people.
At one time I lived with one for three months and a half
    without knowing he was one, since we were old friends . . .
I cannot say how one becomes a member of the secret group
    or what excludes one.
Admission is bound to be ruled by an elaborate code.
I do not also know how one can leave such a group; this might
    be trickier.
I do not also know how one can convince his friends that he is no
    longer a *luwang lwak*, this is the trickiest.

Kabeke's 'Return

The season was dry; a hunting party was in progress.
The hunting area was ringed with fire
All the surrounded game were dead before their death.
Kabeke who had himself arranged the holocaust came late, lost
    his way, and was doomed.
With his fatal band, he saw the flames approaching:
And to the winds he cast his last breath:

  Life lives in the atmosphere like chemicals.
  It is inhaled into the child and given out at death.
  And man is a walking chemical bubble
  Tied down by blood, bones, and flesh: other chemicals all.
  Man himself is one: a cactus tree.
  Its branches are strewn all over where they behaved chameleon.
  The amoeba breaks with life in fractions.
  A piece of magnet is polarized.
  There once lived a manandwoman creature.
  From himher other menandwomen broke off.
  For ease of mobility man and woman became,
  With woman keeping the scabbard and man taking the lance.
  But for fractionalization itthey manandwoman again and again
  The factors can manwoman in test tubes too.
  Manandwomanandotheranimalsandthings broke off a tree;
  The tree broke off humid ground.
  Wait for this hot chemical to reach your chemicals.
  You affect the fire as much as it affects you.
  Only Fear and Pain are daughters of education.
  While true laughter is not.
  What we call knowledge is a chemical substance.
  According to the combinations and preponderance in
    your glands and nerves and corpuscles
  You have an affinity for similar chemicals
  I am made of fire so with fire I shall unite.

Raole 'Banyale[1]

In Madi there once lived a man named Raole.
Advanced in years, he now sat at home with children of sons.
One morning the sun was sharp and his appetite was up.
The smell of food was good and he took a walk before lunch.
Where the road forked an eagle flirted above.
Out of its gripping claws a piece of flesh fell.
Raole, as near hungry as the eagle, raced for it.
With luck unluck he grabbed it first
And dusted away at the liver a hand in size.
He went home and lit a fire outside for a roast.
What reached his nose made his mouth water.
With salt added he swallowed fast what children should have
    eaten.
The liver became smaller and smaller while his appetite
    increased in size.
The last swallowing was the beginning of an era of hunger.
Off Raole went where the roads fork:
Perchance another eagle might bring the heavenly food.
But, no, Raole, no more gift from those who fly.
For, whoever knows where eagles hunt,
What they catch and the gifts they bring?

Days came and days went. Raole had a life new.
No more stay-at-home but a hunter of livers he became.
An eland he killed, a zebra he speared, the giraffe's long neck
    he flattened low:
But none of these had the liver the eagle had brought so
    ominously.
With the passage of time, couldn't the tempo of hunting
    increase?
When there was desperation, didn't his temper rise?
When the hunter is thirsty, can thirst go away unquenched?

So a new moon came and Raole slept out with a dog, nets and
  spears.
But all the livers he ate were diluted or flat.
Till one day he retraced his steps and arrived where the roads
  fork.
He stood still and thought he saw his eagle.
Homewards it sent its gaze, thence it also flew.
Raole heard a bell, and the path that goes home he also
  followed.

His own sons had gone far to dig;
His daughters had gone to look for fuel and food;
Only the children of sons were around.
The one that greeted him first he detained:
The others he sent to the river to bathe.
With a knife he slit its neck open.
With another he cut the stomach through.
At a second he ripped the liver quickly.
At a jump the liver was already roasting.
And he ate before he hid the corpse.
And —
But this was the liver the eagle had brought.

The other children returned and felt an absence.
The daughters returned and called a silence.
The fathers returned and asked a question.
Only 'Banyale sat unconcerned. Or so they thought.
But where the liver was he knew for sure. Not where life went.
People grumbled but had nothing proving.
I wish they had seen what the ant-heap had hidden.

Life goes out of man with every cohabitation.
A father sees his sperm grow into a man.

A grandfather sees branches of himself multiplied.
With each cohabitation life goes out of a man.
With each cohabitation a man loses strength.
With every cohabitation a man becomes less man
And hunger for flesh increases when flesh is diminished.
How long will Raole wait before he strikes again?
How long will the children play before they sense a missing?
How long can sons count a number even?
How long will mothers await the pangs of milk unsucked?
Not very long.
For now a month has passed
And 'Banyale strikes tomorrow.

The usual story was told: Raole doesn't know a thing;
This was an act of God and fate's hand rules supreme.
Inwardly Raole wondered if he would ever reform.
Ambiguously he saw thirty bonny children laughing in the court
And 'Banyale conjured up thirty fishes swimming in a pool
    for fishing.
Were these mere fish? No, these were oysters, bearers of pearls.
And what woman ever refused a pearl
When so many could be had for naught?
Which thief ever left a bank
When no detectives were around?
Away! Away, spirit of restraint.
Raole shall have his flesh back
And live a youth times thirty and five.

Today he decides on a selection:
The liver of the girl is bigger as she thinks less;
The liver of the fatted girl is sweeter as it is also fatter.
Raole grips the girl on the neck.
And HARK! the bell tolls!

Raole's teeth are knocked inside!
A son had been on guard since kill number two.
Raole blessed his girl with spits of blood and broken teeth;
His ears ached the more as blows rained on blows:
He cried like the child he had grown into.

It was the evening of the last day when the elders met
And postponed the fate of their father a day more
Since in the morn the court was to fill with judges
And Raole's incest broadcast abroad.

With the hair of a beast and the gift of a bird
Can Raole ever await the morn to come?
With the suspicions of a thief and the wits of a killer
Can Raole ever give his subnormal foes a chance?
Those who thought Raole was old would see.
Those who thought Raole was unloved would see.
For, before the first waking, Raole was up;
Before husbands had consumed a kiss he was about;
Before food had reached the fart Raole woke his cousin;
Before the girl had scratched her swelling neck
'Banyale and his sister's sons were gone —
And gone for good – or evil!

Labek, Dibe, and the Abayo Meteorite[1]

Between Palabek and Padibe there is a place called Akwang
And in this place there is a hill called Abayo
Which fell from the heavens mysteriously burying many
    bacchanals.

Sex and fun-loving Labek and Dibe were runaway sons of
    Jule of Pajule.
They so loved sex that they behaved like brutes: chasing girls
    and women as if they were cows or bitches in heat
Without the slightest realization that morals divide man from
    beasts.
(But perhaps as happens with most sex maniacs, they were
    acting under a complex:
Sufferers from masochism: therefore loving to inflict pain on
    woman as well as on themselves during orgasms.
Loving humiliation as they court and receive the inevitable
    social jeers;
As well as suffering from sadism since they get pleasure from
    this feminine cruelty.
All considered, man inflicts pains on himself and other
    organisms when he is shying away from a fundamental
    challenge, or seeking to bury a guilt within his
    subconscious.
So sex is the pain of birth-throes, although other pilgrims fall
    foul to its bitter-sweet allurements.
Others sharpen their sexual sensitivities, so that much sex is
    their medicine as is the case with drug addicts.
Sex is the refuge of weaklings.)
In where Got Abayo now stands Dibe and Labek went to a
    dance:
Everybody imbibed the mania for sex so infused
So that promiscuity passed all the orgies:

The dancers were many, so were the lookers on, and grass was
    crushed to bits as huts were now full.
More beer was to be drunk to cloud the vision
Girls had to get some water as the pots were empty
At the well they found a man who spoiled their vision:
The toes and fingers were gone and dripping lymph
His skin had frogged and he looked a leper perfect.
'My God!' one of the girls blurted and spat in disgust.
Yet the apparition felt his way towards the beauties
Who half-filled their pots in a jitter and would not give him
    water.
'We cannot give you our vessels,' said the whole ones.
'You will soil them, or worse, infect them,' one of them
    declared.
'And we have to take water to our lovers,' insisted another.
'Reach the water in the well with your mouth, you bugger!'
    another concluded.
The leper's wounds dripped the more
As his eyes started shedding tears.
He nursed his double wound and retreated back to his lair.

Thirst is thirst and cannot be squashed by wrath alone.
This man saw another batch of carousers coming for more.
He hesitated to approach but at last went to them.
The girls had been briefed and their invectives defy the pen.
The man argued within himself that he did not invite the
    plague:
He too had parents and relatives enough who might be making
    fun now;
He was the son of man but society declared him an outcast.
At whose door must he now lay his grief?

He asked the river god for judgement and the slippery one
    recommended extinction.
But before retribution fell they needed a witness and a
    repository of the annals.
A single girl came crying to the well cast out by her mates:
The crying fugitives helped each other for ever:
Our humble girl washed clean her *agwata*[2] and got the clearest
    water for her leper;
The friend quenched his thirst and blessed the kind one.
He begged her to go remove from dance her kindred
As the wrath of God would rain on the sinners.
She went and collected all believers.
But those who doubted remained to perish.
And then the sky decided to fall: darkness encompassed the
    horizon.
A blanket of rock descended on humans, and pounded all
    beneath the surface.

The Birth of Heartbeat

[For Lubuc, Dingidingi Captain of Uganda's Heartbeat of
Africa, one of the greatest dancers of century twenty.[1]]

The rain spears fell, pat, pat, pat, pat, breaking into flood.
The anthill tops were softened. Two days later, the worker
ants had cut exits for the season's white-ant generation to fly
forth into the world and perhaps meet a mate and build
another subterranean city vaulted high.

Apwoyo[2] and his wife Min-Obuthe,[3] got ready for a catch
of the delicious edibles. Torches out of dry grass they made.
Two anthills they netted with grass roof. One hill was on this
side of the river to be tended by Min-Obuthe, and the other
on that side to be tended by Won-Obuthe himself.

After the evening meal, Apwoyo grabbed his pile of torches,
duty-bound, and rushed off for the catch. He arrived there to
find the worker-ants had already cleared many channels to let
the lovely fresh, and ever-clean ants out. And the lovely, fat,
clean, beautifully-clad-in-white-wings-only ants were hurrying
out to try out their new wings, breathe fresh air, and see how
the world was. Apwoyo lit his torch, and ants hurried out in
millions to see the new-found light. Alas, they were duped
to fall into the collection hole, where they were doomed for
Apwoyo's table. Apwoyo's appetite was worked up: he was
all a-tremble at this sign of plenty. Okolok, the millipede,
had also come near the anthill. He, the master musician,
prepared himself for a song. His multicorded harp was tuned,
and Okolok spread his whole length on the breadth of the
harp, and his million legs became playing hands; some for
strumming and others for modulation. He sprung his song,
and sweet music oozed out from between his scales:

Kiri-li-kijii-jii-jii, kirili-kijii[4];
Obala[5] ma yang balo kot ngwen;

94

Kiri-li-kijii:
Obala ma yang balo ngwenna;
Kot ngwen cwer, cwer, cwer;
Obala ma yang balo kot ngwen!

Kiri-li-kijii-jii-jii, kirilili-kijii;
Obala who is used to letting white ants fly away;
Kiri-li-kijii;
Obala who is used to letting white ants fly away
Rain, rain, white ant rain, rain
Obala who is used to letting white ants fly away.

Straightaway, Apwoyo pricked up his large ears. He heard,
as if he hadn't heard. But Okolok had only paused to clear
his throat, to watch the effect of his music on Apwoyo the
master dancer. Okolok shook his ankle bells: *kiri-li-ki-jii-jii,
kirili-kijii.* And Apwoyo threw down his dead torch. He
snatched his dancing axe, and was poised for a dance. Okolol
went on: *Kiri-li-kijii* . . . Apwoyo was roused to dance: his
hand was up, axe brandishing; the other hand kept the
rhythm; his neck oscillated his head, the backbone became
suppled; the hip joint dangled his legs like some weird puppets.
He danced, and danced, and was wet with sweat. His sweat
fell like fireworks, against the bright moonlight and the myriad
gyrating ants.

Kalang the black ant helped Okolok with the song.
Apwoyo did the dance. Already an hour had passed and
Apwoyo was still in the throes of dance-perfection.

All the ants were out: in the air. Then Kalang stopped
singing. And Okolok moved with his harp away. Apwoyo
stopped: saw and he could not see. Where were the ants? Up
in the air! Or crawling on the ground, where an army of
Kalang was having a rich catch, where Okolok was busy
grabbing a million ants at a time!

Apwoyo, what will you do when you get back home?
Without even a handful of ants for your Min-Obuthe, yes,
Min-Obuthe the termagant, your henpecker? And what will
you take to the greedy-eyed Obuthe? Undoubtedly, Apwoyo
pulled a trick out of his fertile hat. The remaining torches, he
put over his shoulder; the axe on the other. Then, left-right,
left-right, he wended his way home. In the river between,
Apwoyo fully immersed himself in the water: torches and
all . . . He climbed out, and shook the extra water out of his
scooping ears and jata, jata, jata, he hurried home. Fifteen
more yards to reach home; fifteen more yards to perfect a lie;
fifteen more yards to face a virago; fifteen more yards to
confront the hungry looks of a devouring child . . .

Apwoyo: 'Min-Obuthe! Min-Obuthe! I say, Min-Obuthe?
Wake up. Wake up. Wife, are you dreaming or what. Wake up!'

Such an earnest note assured Min-Obuthe that, at least for
once, her husband had come home a husband, a father, a man:
provident.

Min-Obuthe: 'Wake up. Wake up. Obuthe, I say, wake up!'
She shook their son, 'Your father has come back. Heavy.'

'Min-Obuthe. Min-Obuthe. Wake up. Get me a fire ready.
I am almost dead, dead with cold. Help. Help. Help. Help,
wife, sister, help. I am dead, cold, cold, cold, is killing me.
And hunger.'

All agape at the sight of her wet husband, Min-Obuthe
exclaimed: 'Ah, Apwoyo, when did it rain? The sky is all
clear!' 'O! O! O! O! Wife, sister, don't say like that. The rain,
the rain, that rain which fell on the other side of the river was
enough to melt you. Look, look look – see, see how wet I
am? see how up my skin stands? There was wind . . . do you
speak of wind? There was hail . . . hail stones . . . haa, haa, I
cried and cried . . . ran and ran. No. You shouldn't joke. I
tried to run but could not move an inch: I ran on the same

spot. I ran forward the wind blew me backwards. Thank our god I am still alive. Come on, get me some food. You can't keep me here standing, starving, shivering, without thinking of help. You ungrateful wife, you want me, your husband to die of hunger? As if hails and wind were not deaths enough.' Min-Obuthe lit the fire and Won-Obuthe repaired there to warm himself and sharpen his appetite for the food his wife was setting before him. Apwoyo ate, and ate, ate and ate, ate and ate till he could eat no more, till he had recovered his lost energy, till he had stored enough food for breakfast. He then lay down, and slept. Slept flat till the sun was up.

The following day, Won- and Min-Obuthe, got ready many more torches. That done, Apwoyo, with more alacrity and energy than was manifest in making the torches, got his dancing shield out and cleaned it; got his head gear out and tried the ostrich feathers on; smoothed his leopard skin for the dance; his armband with giraffe tail was combed; the blowing horn was emptied of webs with oil on feathers. Obala who leaves the ants go moved with the kel kel of desire for the dance, desire for the supremest of dances ... the dance of weddings.

'Won-Obuthe, how is it today? Where is the dance? The dance you don't tell people about?' Mrs Apwoyo asked.

'No. No. No. There is no dance, wife. If there were a dance, do you think I wouldn't have told you about it? I don't behave like that. I am just getting my things ready for the day, the day of the big dance. So that on that day I don't run about like an idiot. Moreover, these things need cleaning once in a while, don't you think so?'

She thought so. She was reassured ...

Evening came. The sun went. Apwoyo could not wait for

food. He nicely folded up the leopard skin. The headgear and the feathers, and horn, and arm-band, and all the dancing costumes, were packed in the basket, while wife and son were unaware. As he had been so fortunate the other night, to meet with a god-sent dance, he had better go early today. As he had been so unfortunate last night as to be beaten by the rain, he told his wife he had better go early today. Min-Obuthe agreed. Obuthe saw his father off. And teng, teng, teng, teng with his ears, Apwoyo hurried off to . . .

Fifteen yards away from son, fifteen yards away from his wife, fifteen yards away from home, Apwoyo threw the torches down. The basket was lowered to the ground. The dancing costumes got out and were worn into place: headgear on head, waistband on waist, ankle bells on, ting, ting, ting, the dancer went. The hunter, the father, the husband, was all left behind.

Okolok was ever vigilant. To despoil Apwoyo's hunt of ants he was all prepared; to benefit from Apwoyo's mischance was his primary design: the ants which eventually return to the ground were his to dig up. To get all the ants for his family, or that of Kalang, he was ready to sing his heart out. *Kiri-li-kijii* . . . And Apwoyo broke out into his dancing cry:

> *Awod Olel,*[6] *Awod jo Olel*
> *Tin rac tin, tin rac tin*
> *Awod Obala, Awod Obala*
> *Obala ma weko ngwen duny.*
> I'm Olel's son, I'm Olel's son
> What an opportunity, what an opportunity,
> I'm Obala's son, I'm Obala's son
> Obala who lets the ants fly away.

And he blew the horn. And he danced and danced. And he sweated a whole lake.

The cocks crowed; the Okolok gave no encore; Kalang
got the cue, other men went home with baskets full of ants,
Apwoyo dragged his feet home.

His wife had taken care of the hill near home. Her collection
filled baskets two.

Apwoyo arrived home wet. He growled a lot. His wife did
not ask a thing. She did not believe enough.

Her husband warmed himself up, fed himself on his wife's
earlier catch, and was tucked to bed.

And then Min-Obuthe went to see what Apwoyo hid in
the basket. She covered it up again, very well, very well!

Apwoyo woke up on the morrow and was fed with
porridge. Then he waited till his wife was away before he
went to dry the dancing costume.

The following evening Apwoyo rushed off to catch ants.
Perhaps he thought this would be his last dance before he got
down to serious business, before he was called to account for
his behaviour. Perhaps he did not even think these thoughts.
Anyway, he started.

And his wife was not far behind.

Fifteen yards to go, he announced his arrival:

Awod pa Obala, Awod pa Obala
Awod pa dako matidi, awod pa dako matidi
Awod pa Kiteng teng.
I am Obala's son, I am Obala's son
I'm the younger wife's son, I'm the younger wife's son
The son of he who walks Kiteng teng.

And off he ran to attack the ant-hill.
Okolok heard and had not heard. The harp was now played
by the moving wind. Black Orpheus was busy at work! *Kiri
kiri* began that very night.

'Who has ever counted the feet of the millipede?
Or enjoyed the undulating poetry of their movement?
These were the feet that served as hands
When she struck the tune on her multicorded harp
And the song vibrated through all her scales.'

Kalang sang for the angels and trees. Ants followed the
pipers! Meanwhile, the ants were flying up in swarms. To
Apwoyo there were definitely more dancers than one. Or was
he deceived? Or was he deceived? Before him he could see
male dancers. Or what were they? And weren't they
interlocked? Weren't those white *girikots*[7] that lapped at their
buttocks? How does that headgear bob? No, whatever these
are, they are welcome. The more the merrier. The dance
continued, better than before. There was that percussion of
the wire on the calabash: *cheke, cheke, cheke, cheke*. And
suddenly it stopped. And then feet and voices gave us the
music. And then the silent music of mime and body rhythm
takes over. There was a boy bright and fierce: there was a girl
slim and tall and beauteous. The boy sought the girl's eyes.
The girl gave him all she could. But up in the heavens, the
atmosphere was thick: thick with ants. Ants gyrating towards
the moon. The moon could scarcely reach the ground for the
lamokowang[8] dance. The moon herself yearned to come and
get stuck. To a pole.
  Boys and girls danced. While their hearts filled with
beauty, their nostrils dilated with fire.

The ripe breasts begged for picking and yet sought their
    mistress.
Like the leaf in the glade who can count her movement?
Like the ripple in the river who can divine her movement?
Like the legs of the millipede who can count their motions?

When the Nile waters cascade down the falls who dares
    analyse their movements?
When a spasm begins from toes and head who can be sure
    of the meeting place?
When the chest was forwards-backwards the stomach was
    backwards-forwards.
And the waist was neither forwardsbackwards. . . .
Who can be sure whether there was a neck a spine or a waist?
Indeed, who can be sure whether there was a girl at all?
And then when she danced from side to side she was a
    moving target.
A Hunter wouldn't know where the bull's eye hid . . .
He might have ended up salivating in utter frustration.
Apwoyo became the dance.
And then tragedy struck.

Apwoyo's heart fell. He thought he saw a lovely sweetheart
of his youth dancing by him, before him, on the other side of
the hill. Up and down. He thought he had a mate whose feet
floated on a cushion of air; whose feet were neither left nor
right: whose legs were loose at the joints. He really thought
the girl had no waist at all but a supple movability. Didn't
she really have beads on her waist and a skirt to vibrate?
Wasn't her backbone a flame to flicker? And her hands,
didn't they dance apart from the dancing frame? Her neck
had beads, he was sure, but was it human, really human?
Didn't it toss the head about like some mad seal in pleasure?
And what did that face look like? Where had he seen it
before? Hark! The mist disappeared from his eyes. He shook
his head. Reality faced him, in the solid frame of his wife, the
termagant Min-Obuthe. The Okolok sensed the tension. The
Kalang saved their voices. Min-Obuthe fixed her gaze.
    Apwoyo brought up the excuse: 'Min-Obuthe. Min-Obuthe.

Don't get me wrong ...'

'*Twa twaca, twa twaca, twa twac twac twac* .... You will see today, you good for nothing thing. You keep me hungry, you kill your own son with hunger, and come here merely for a dance ... today you will see!' And Apwoyo, who could not stand up against his wife; Apwoyo who could not stand his wife, for sure ... he ran, and ran ... ran and ran, ran till he formed the heartbeat'![9]

NOTES

SPEARS, BEADS, BEANS AND OTHERS

THE SPEAR, BEAD AND BEAN STORY

Pan-Lwo. The outline of this legend is known to every Lwo speaker.
Names and number of the major characters, and locations of the
actions vary. The Alur versions are the most embellished. In fact,
among the Lwo, the Alur have the most imaginative and elaborate
versions of Lwo mythologies.

This is not only a narration but also an attempt at a new interpretation
of the mythological language in which the story is couched. I have
also added a few conjectures of my own.

If these legends are to live, they must be made contemporary.

1 *Gipir* or *Lapir* (Acholi) – He who revenges, the avenger.
2 *Labongo* (Acholi) – He who lacks, or who is without (power,
wealth, etc).
3 *Peke* – durable dry foods for a traveller.
4 *Min Lyec* – Elephant Mother, A huge, elephantine woman.
5 *Nyambogo* – *Mbogo* is a Bantu word meaning 'Buffalo'.
   Nya is Lwo word for 'Daughter'.
6 *Ngor Lwo* – Lwo peas, (ancestral).
7 *Tiku Burjok* – Big blue beads (hole or ulcer of god).
8 *Aba Mara* – My father loves me.
9 *Jok* – God (Juogh, Juagh, Jehova, Yehova, Yahweh, Zeus,
Deus?)

10 The prototype river of this mythology has not been clearly identified.
The Nile is a likely candidate, but how come Sudanic and Nilo–Hamitics
(some Bantu-speakers have bits and pieces of it as integral parts of their
traditions) also have the story?

11 Although this mythological character-revelation has been appropriated
by the Lwo, it is also common among the Sudanic people and the so-called
Half-Hamites: Masai, etc. It is possible that these groups were 'brothers'
in the distant past, and are therefore preserving the history, or circumstances
of their break in this very involved language. This is just a conjecture. But
the tribes which acted it out first, or originated this story, or appropriated
it for themselves, have found in it the best revelation of their tribal sub-
conscious.

THE LOST TRIBES
Alur.

1 *Jwok* or *Jok*, or *Juogh* – God, spirit.

2 Slaves whose functions were taking care of the palatial and clan Gods.

3 The Spear (Labongo's that the elephant carried away), and the knife (with which the child's stomach was split open), caused their extinction.

NYILAK, THE FAMOUS GIRL OF THE PLAINS
Alur. Nyilak's child was a boy named Opodho, an Alur and Luo common ancestor.

1 Rwot (Chief, King) Lei (Animals (?)

2 *Lak* or *lak* – roam, wander. Nyilak – the child (in this case, girl) who roams, or wanders, or looks after cows in the plains.

3 The Lwo are not hairy. This creature must have been markedly hairy and a stranger. Or is it an Esau-Jacob type of deception?

4 *Cak* – begin. *Ocak* – he who begins.

5 *Koth, Kot* – rain. (Koth was also a god.)

GODS FAVOUR THOSE BORN TO BE KINGS
Madi, Bari and Acholi. Non-Lwo tribes have versions of this story.

THERE IS AN OLD KIND LADY IN LWO MYTHOLOGY
Alur. The Kind Lady, without a name except in one or two cases, plays general rescue work to the helpless and afflicted. It was she who gave Gipir his lost spear. In this story, she is doing exactly what Pharaoh's daughter did with Moses. It may even be that this is the Lwo version of the same Biblical story. Somewhere in the distant past the Lwo and other East African tribes might have had connections with the Middle East. Evidence is gathering.

1 Nyilak, the most famous Lwo girl in these stories features in many legends, sometimes under different names.

2 Normally the first twin is called Opiyo (the fast one) and the second Ocen (the one who remained behind), the next child is Okello (he who brought up the twins' rear) and Odong comes next. Twins and wonder children and other peculiarly born or formed children were most times destined for leadership. But there are times when death is their sentence for being so peculiar.

3 Apparently, those detailed to kill, had feared shedding blood and had therefore thrown the babes into the stream so that the river would bear the responsibility for this homicide, however non-humans twins are. And from this stream our dear old lady had collected them.

4 To point at somebody's eyes in anger, even with the finger alone, is symbolic murder.

5 This Odongo, sometimes called Cwa, is mentioned as the father of Gipir, Tipol, Nyabongo, and Kamarasi. Cwa may be a corruption of Shoa of Ethiopia, an area whose memory has not disappeared long after centuries of migration.

OCUDHO OF KIR
Anywah.

1 Cuai, or Chwa, or Cua, is a common name of people or places among the Lwo and even Bari-speakers. This is possibly the strongest link between the Lwo and Shoa in Ethiopia where they may have originated or passed through. (See note at end of last story.)

2 We are people of Cuai.

3 To migrants, justice or fairness is a cardinal principle. The just are elected leaders or rulers.

4 Stone quiet.

5 Is Nyairu Nyilak?

6 In those early days, it was easier for wonderful or mysterious guests or foreigners to marry princesses and inherit the thrones. Or their children definitely became kings.

RWOT LEI
Alur.

1 *Lei* = Animal (?)

2 Is this a version of the Esau-Jacob story?

3 The inner part of a hut or house.

4 The royal drum.

MALKAL, KAL PA MAL, MALAKAL
Anywah.

1 Malakal is a corruption of Mal's *Kal* – Mal's palace.

2 *Mal* – to wander or move about, it also means 'up'.

3 Gourd = or Ker, or Pumpkin. Okono has never left the Lwo psyche. Okot p'Bitek's popular *Song of Lawino* is an injunction, 'Thou shalt not uproot the Old Pumpkin.'

4 Mal is reputed to have received a divine spear from up. These spears!

5 *Nam:* River (large one) or lake. Is Lolwe presaged?

6 The word for friend in Acholi is *Larema:* the one with whom I share blood, by ceremoniously drinking or exchanging it.

NYIKANGO AND DAK

Collo. Deep religious mythologies of the Middle Eastern fashion among the Lwo are almost only found among the Collo. With these long-ago hazy narratives, I have attempted to keep the dream flavour.

1 Cang = Sun

2 Nyikango is the most famous of Lwo heroes, rivalled by the girl, Nyiak. Dak is Nyikango's 'son' as well as rival. Nyikango, or Okang (Acholi) is the first boy born to his parents. Is this Nyikango 'The First Man'?

3 Is Dak a sort of Bacchus?

4 The function of the boar in Greek and other Eastern mythologies.

5 Collo were commoners. This is the possible evolution of aristocracy among them.

NYIKANGO AND DHIMO

Collo. Some of the story's surrealism is preserved.

1 Dhimo must have been a great artist.

2 Here two brothers separated on account of spear and fish. Hunting game in the bush or hunting fish in the river is a Lwo speciality, as well as a cause of friction!

DAK AND DHIMO

Collo. The leaps in time and logic have been preserved in order to retain the magical flavour.

1 Dak also means 'migration' in Acholi.

2 There must have been great sculptors in Collo land. Already from ambatch wood an exact fish has been made and here we have a realistic representation of Dak.

3 You cannot go across a boundary marked by blood.

HOW NYIKANGO WENT TO HEAVEN

Collo.

1 The supreme God among the Collo. He lives up in heaven.

2 Rain, Sun, and Rivers feature a lot in early Lwo stories. They must

have lived in a dry, rainless country near a river. This is the only known case of a Lwo ascending to heaven. There are Middle Eastern characteristics in this story.

THE COMING OF LOMUKU'DIT
Bari. Father Crazzolara postulates that this Bari legend records the passing of the Lwo southwards through Nimule. On the other hand it could have applied to the other hordes who went south and who are not Lwo. Some of these routes were well-known in ancient times and well-used. Greeks and Romans used them before the later European explorers of the last century. Africans who were explorers, colonizers, and migrants southwards in their own rights. also used them in their time.

Part Two

EATING CHIEFS

THE FIRST KING IN THE WORLD
Acholi and Lango.
  1 Duiker.
  2 This is one of the most ancient myths in Lwo.

APWOYO, LAGUT, KA OBI – THE HARE, THE GUY AND THE OGRE
Acholi version.
This is an example of strategy in capturing new territories.
  1 The smith has attracted food.
  2 A stringed musical instrument.
  3 Go and never return.

BILO NYUKA – TASTING PORRIDGE
Alur and Reli.
  1 That seasoned blacksmiths should have asked for extra fire is another thing altogether.
  2 Before he died, my father told me a version of the same.
Reli's son actually said: 'My father sent me to taste the porridge:
                            If the porridge is cold, I should drink it;
                            But if it is hot, I must call for him!'
  3 Another example of strategy for colonization.

Notes

KIDNAPPED

Alur.

1 *Yudo* a term for whisking fish out of water. Here it is given the meaning of abduction.

2 Greatness is thrust upon those who deserve it.

THE PATH OF REASON IS A TWISTED THING

Alur.

TAMING THE SAVAGES

Alur. Many savage tribes came under Lwo rule in order to be better fed. They wanted security from hunger. Lwo sections also hived off to join other tribes for the same reason.

1 Bread.

BRIGHTNESS IS ITSELF A CURSE

Acholi. This is a recent story.

1 Clerks.

TYPES OF REASONING

Alur.

1 The people make the kings and keep them when they are responsible and respectful. The people unmake the kings when these kings misuse their powers or forget their duties.

2 *'Kiling . . .* – onomatopoeic representation of the drum sound. Talking drums are not facets of Lwo and other East African tribes as is the case with West Africa.

THE BIRTH OF KAMALEGA

Alur. The Alur, as well as other Central and Southern Lwo, have strong traditions which bind them with the Bunyoro and other Bantu kingdoms in Uganda.

OBURA THE JUST

Pawir and Acholi.

1 Fine for making a girl pregnant before marriage.

2 A foreigner "from across the Nile" – south of Atura. Generally, it means a Muntu.

3 Justice and fairness were greatly prized.

DEAD GIRAFFE'S REVENGE
Pawir and Acholi.

1 The tail hairs of the giraffe. These are still highly prized for making necklets and wristlets.

2 *Ayaa, Maayaa, An do, Wiido, Eii* are expressions of grief, surprise, wonder.

3 *Dogo* – bark cloth.

4 *Oyo opilo* – a tiny tawny-striped rat.

BURA LEB BARI
Padhola.

1 *Bura* is from Bari Language. It has to do with royalty, palace, custom, court.

2 Wonder-workers usually ended up on the throne, though sometimes there are cases where they ended up at the stake or in exile.

A RECENT OCCURRENCE
Lwo.

1 Provincial Commission.

2 God.

3 The Sky; also a kind of spirit.

4 From the Luganda word meaning a foreigner different, tribesman.

Part *Three*

OK ICHIEM GI WADWU

'Thou shalt not commune with thine brethren.' In the things that matter in life, the Luo are governed by this teaching rather than the superficial, untragic 'Eat with your brother – *Chiem gi wadwu.*'

ANGULU
Lango and Acholi, Madi and Alur, Bunyoro and Teso, Kumam and Karamojong, and Kuku, for a change.

1 Whom have they speared? They have killed our Angulo! Oh God, our Great Angulo is dead!

2 War Leader, Field Marshal.

3 Hamlet or Subclan.

4 Pollute not the present generation with their grand-parents' iniquities.

KOP BINO MA IKWIYA – FATE STRIKES WITHOUT WARNING
Acholi.
  1 Heroic praise – name.
  2 Tomahawk, or axe.
  3 *Ayaa* – an address of sorrow or helplessness.
  4 A tree.
  5 Army, fighters.

THE UKEBU, IRON, MEROE, AND LWO
Alur.
  The Ukebu are a Lwo-conquered tribe. As with many conquered and absorbed tribes, they had a tribal trade, in this case, blacksmithery, whose tricks they kept a secret. How did the Ukebu become blacksmiths?
  1 Highland Alur.

THE BIRTH OF AN EXODUS
Southern Madi and Alur. The Pojulu and Reli are Bari-speaking tribes. Sections of these groups have been blended with the Central and Southern Lwo. This narrative illustrates one of the methods of hiving off.

EXCAVATION SITES
Acholi.
  1 Cave-men
  2 Communal work, in this case, digging.
  3 Bread.
  4 Beer.
  5 Mr A. B. Adimola has treated the Lamogi War against the British in his article 'Lamogi Rebellion' in *Uganda Journal*.
  6 Practically all African migrants have stories of encounter with these little people whom they walled up in caves, or who disappeared underground, or who were driven farther south into the depths of the forests, or the heights of the mountains.

LACEK OBALO KAKA
Acholi.
  1 Duiker

2 Clan.

3 White ants.

4 Red askari ants.

5 A wild beast's baby.

6 Edible rat.

7 The front leg of a game traditionally offered to the clansman.

8 Many delicious grasshoppers. These were royal food. By Appointment, His Highness the Kabaka, and other chiefs.

9 Fat.

UNU ME TWEYO CUN
Lango and Acholi.

1 *Jo* = People (clan); *Won*[2] = Father (of); *Min*[3] = Mother (of); *Ladit*[4] = Chief, Lord.

5 Wealth, especially bride wealth.

6 Daughter of.

7 This is an example of building up a legend from a clan name. There are Gem groups in Alur, and Lwo who never descended from this Okulla.

OMERA, CIP AYE OTERA ITIM
Acholi and Lango.

1 My brother, it is only because I was born a woman that I have to look for a home in foreign lands.

2 Traditional female apron (also connoting the female principle).

3 Traditional male loin-cloth (also connoting the male principle).

4 (a) – female principle (my).

5 A derogatory word for an old bachelor. Traditionally, a man who remained a bachelor for a long time was almost a woman. Those men who were destitute and could not obtain wealth for brideprice ended up taking over their deceased brother's and other relatives' wives. A son could also inherit his father's younger wives.

6 Abwoc was a Lango girl who had to run away to Acholi.

TO YOU CRAZZOLARA
Acholi.

1 The Famine of the Lions. Periods of famine were given names depending on the causes, and effects of the famine. The famine could also be named after other memorable events which took place during it.

2 Commoners' offerings to the aristocrats or Chiefs.

3 Foreign or secret language.

KALABARA'S DAMP SORE
Acholi and Pawir. There are many versions of this story among the
Lwo and other tribes with different names and places. Some of the
stories are more ancient than this. Don't judge by appearances; as you
treat others you may also be rewarded.

THE DIVISION OF LABOUR AMONG THE PARI
1 Pari (Acholi of Sudan).
2 The plight of women was better here than that of men or women
in any other Lwo group. Circumstances govern social choices and
regulations.

YOM CWINY ONEKO LATINA
Lango and Acholi version.
1 Hospitality is also deadly.
2 Beer.
3 Yeast.
4 Calabashful.
5 In the traditional stories Latina is a man. It adds more pathos to
make her a woman.

LUWANG LWAK
Pari (Acholi of Sudan).
1 Vigilantes.
2 Mixing the old and the new.

KABEKE'S RETURN
Pajok (Acholi of Sudan).
This contains the new in the old.

RAOLE 'BANYALE
Madi, and Lwo.
1 There is much of a Promethean tragedy here. Grace Ogot has
already treated a version of this story in an excellent short story
called 'Tekayo'.

LABEK, DIBE, AND THE ABAYO METEORITE
Acholi.
1 There are other 'nationalized' or 'regionalized' versions of

this story among the Lwo and non-Lwo. What are the differences
between this and 'Kalabara's Damp Shore'? For a sister legend, read
footnote 42, Chapter 5, of Professor B. A. Ogot's *History of the Southern
Lwo*, vol. I. A historical meteorite might have originated these stories.
Vesuvius.

  2 Calabash.

THE BIRTH OF HEARTBEAT

Acholi. I am indebted to Okot p'Bitek for the outline of this story.
Ants, grasshoppers, game hunting, fishing betray too much
dependence on nature's bounty for Lwo livelihood in times past as
contrasted with the pastoral Masai or Hima.

  1 Miss Lubuc is the Captain of the Lwo section of the Uganda
Heartbeat of Africa. Without doubt she is the best dancer I have seen.

  2 Hare.

  3 Apwoyo has a wife called 'Mother of Obuthe'. Obuthe is their
only known son.

  4 Onomatopoeia for ankle – bell music.

  5 Obala – derogatory praise name for 'He who wastes' (white ants)
or lets white ants fly away uncollected.

  6 *Olel*, broth or other soups made with simsim or groundnut paste.

  7 Skin dress worn by male dancers on their buttocks.

  8 Youth's evening dance where wooing and love-making take place.

  9 Every great artist is as impractical, lazy, unconscious of his duties
and family responsibilities, and social commitment as Obala. Artists
dance while the ants are flying. We sing while the sensible ones are
collecting hay and amassing wealth. Pray for us poor souls. *Awod
Obala!*